BETH CHATTO'S

Green Tapestry

BETH CHATTO'S

Green Tapestry

HarperCollins*Illustrated*

HarperCollins*Illustrated* is an imprint of
HarperCollins*Publishers* Ltd
77-85 Fulham Palace Road
London W6 8JB

The HarperCollins website address is:
www.**fire**and**water**.com

Beth Chatto's Green Tapestry
was conceived by
Anthony Paul, Susan Berry and Steven Wooster
For Duane Paul Design Team,
Unit 30, Ransome's Dock, 35 Parkgate Road,
London SW11 4NP

First published in 1989
by William Collins Sons and Co Ltd
Hardback edition reprinted 1989, 1990, 1994, 1995
by HarperCollins*Publishers*
This paperback edition published 1999

99 01 03 02 00
2 4 6 8 9 7 5 3 1

British Library Cataloguing in Publication Data
Chatto, Beth
Beth Chatto's Green Tapestry
i. Perennial plants in gardening – Great Britain
I Title
635

ISBN 0 00 414064 8

Printed and bound in Hong Kong by Printing Express Ltd.

Photographs: **Ron Sutherland** and **Steven Wooster**
Illustrations: **Madeleine David** Editor: **Penny David**
Editorial assistant: **Sue George** Editorial director: **Susan Berry**
Design: **Steven Wooster**

CONTENTS

Foreword

ALTHOUGH I AM known to many keen gardeners through my nursery, my books and my exhibitions at the Chelsea Flower Show, I am well aware that my name is not familiar to most new gardeners, and it is for them, as much as for those who already know something of my plants and planting and have often expressed their desire for illustrations of them, that I have produced this book.

My garden, which forms the basis of this book, lies in a corner of south-east England that has the lowest rainfall in Great Britain – an average of 50cm/20in a year, falling equally between winter and summer. We often face periods of drought and as watering with hosepipes is usually banned at those times, if I want my plants to survive I do have to grow those that can cope with very dry conditions. Because I cannot grow many of the plants that gardeners living in wetter parts of the British isles grow so easily and well, I have had to go back to the origins of the plants to find those that naturally prefer a low rainfall.

My particular problems were unusual perhaps because the land on which I have made my garden has a range of widely differing conditions. When we started to make the garden, it consisted of several acres of unproductive farm land, with drought-stricken gravel leading down through dense damp, silty, soil into a spring-fed hollow in which lay a narrow ditch. Inspired by my husband Andrew's interest in plant ecology we set about finding plants that would suit these very different, awkward situations. As I explain in the book, we eventually made a Mediterranean garden on the open sunny slopes, planted shade-loving plants beneath the trees, and dammed the spring-fed ditch to provide a home for water-loving plants.

The plants in the different situations come from various appropriate corners of the world. The dry garden has Mediterranean plants, in my pot gardens I use forms of American aloes or agaves to create strong architectural contrast among pots of South African pelargoniums and other tender plants that I overwinter in a frost-free house. Beneath the north-facing walls and in the shady walks I mix woodland plants from Japan, Europe and the States, provided they do not require constant mist and heavy rainfall. Along the margins of the pools I have huge parasols of *Gunnera manicata* from Brazil with the swamp arum, *Lysichitum americanum*, that grows wild in British Columbia.

Although few gardeners with small gardens will experience the range of conditions I did, almost all will face at least some of them. I hope that my own gardening experiences will encourage people to look afresh at their gardens and its particular, often difficult, conditions, like shade or very dry soil or boggy damp places, that they have found so difficult to deal with. I hope they will be able instead to turn them to advantage to grow a range of more interesting plants – those adapted by nature to thrive in such situations. That does not mean that you should not do your best to improve the conditions – by feeding barren soil or by reducing impossibly dense shade. But if you do choose plants appropriate for the conditions, they will repay you by flourishing, harmonizing with each other and requiring little attention, because they are in their appropriate environment. Had you simply chosen your plants because you liked the look of them, regardless of their differing needs, your garden would probably be a sorry mess of wilting and bedraggled plants with very little to link them together.

But it is one thing to choose appropriate plants for the conditions and quite another to arrange them in a pleasing way – something that almost all gardeners, not just novices, find difficult. Although you are helped by choosing plants that naturally grow together, there is much more to it than that. I cannot emphasize enough that the form and shape of the plant and the texture and colour of its leaves are as important as the colour of its flowers. Leaves have a much longer-lasting effect than flowers and can be found in all shapes and sizes and in many shades – not just green but bronze, purple, red and yellow, in more muted colours than flowers. They also contribute many different textures, providing a rich tapestry effect which looks good for much if not all of the growing season. Plants with big bold foliage can create dramatic effects when placed in contrast among smaller-leaved plants. Finally, by the close planting of shrubs and perennial plants you will create a low-maintenance garden since the soil is covered for much of the year with foliage, preventing the germination of weed seedlings.

The shape and form of the whole plant plays an important role in the design – tall plants create good backgrounds and also lift groups of low-growing plants: for example, a fine arching grass planted among low carpeting plants. Apart from the contribution that they make to the overall shape and structure of the planting, big bulky plants with large leaves help to fill any empty spaces, smother weeds and provide shelter for other more delicate plants.

This book gives me the opportunity to share some of the lessons I have learned about the art of planting over the last 30 years as well as to show the results. I hope I have managed to communicate my enthusiasm for the plants themselves, and for perennials in particular, and that you are encouraged, as a result, to think about your planting from a new point of view.

Author's acknowledgments The idea for producing this book came from Anthony Paul, of Duane Paul Design Team, and Susan Berry. It was to be based on a series of conversations between Susan and myself, with the design and some of the photography by Steven Wooster. For me it was a new and interesting approach to writing a book. Susan's overall plan and her role as interested visitor enjoying the garden but wanting to know more about it was the basis on which we worked. I would like to thank Susan and Steven for all the thought and caring work they have put into *The Green Tapestry* which is a credit to them as much as to us, the gardeners at the Beth Chatto Gardens.

I would also like to thank Ron Sutherland for his splendid photographs of my garden, Madeleine David for her delightful illustrations and Penny David for her meticulous editing of the text.

Beth Chatto

Introduction

Alstroemeria aurantiaca tends to be treated as a poor relation of this family since the pink and apricot shades of Alstroemeria ligtu *have become so popular. But well placed, perhaps with white flowers such as* Chrysanthemum maximum, *white lilies or* Achillea ptarmica *'The Pearl' and plenty of fresh green, like these seeding heads of* Euphorbia coralloides, *the strong colour becomes an asset.*

I HAVE LIVED all my life in Essex – I was born in Good Easter near Chelmsford and brought up near Saffron Walden. Gardening, I suppose, is in my blood. My father was a good gardener and my mother too, and even as quite a small child I had a garden of my own. I bought packets of seed and grew annuals. My parents had an interesting garden and grew a number of species plants among the typical collection of cottage garden plants, which in those days was unusual.

After teacher training college during the war, I married Andrew Chatto, a fruit grower. As a child he had lived for several years on the West Coast of America and it was during that time, when he saw Californian poppies (*Eschscholzia*), *Ceanothus* and lupins growing wild, that his interest in plant ecology started. He had previously seen these plants in England and when he saw them in America, his first thought was 'How did all the plants get here?' Much later, I experienced the same kind of surprise when Andrew took me to Switzerland, and it was my turn to have my breath taken away by sheets of flowers growing wild that I had previously only seen cultivated in gardens. The high alps looked like a huge rock garden, grazed short by the cattle and conditioned by the climate. Long rank grass does not grow in the chilled air in thin, shallow soils and these are the ideal growing conditions for plants with small, brilliantly coloured flowers. To see the turf studded with gentians and the rocks covered with cobwebbed houseleeks (*Sempervivum*) and the dry slopes bright with *Dianthus* and many other familiar plants was a revelation.

I think for us both the significance of seeing plants growing together in association and in different situations was what really fired us with the idea of making a garden based on ecological ideas. But when it comes to putting it into practice, you cannot be a complete purist. Gardening is the art of combining plants from

many different areas of the temperate world, to provide pleasure and interest for a much longer season than, say, that of the flowering meadows of the Swiss Alps. Furthermore there are many plants such as stinging nettles or running twitch grass that may be part of a natural association but are not desirable in the garden. However, if I ignore too many of the principles I have learnt from Andrew's teaching and my own observation, either the plants do not perform well or the planting lacks harmony.

We are often surprised by the way the plants themselves do not always grow as we would expect. Something that has astounded my husband is the way I can grow *Helleborus orientalis*. He read that they grow wild in the Caucasus, in and around the foothills in mountainous country, among bushes and trees. When I first put them in an open site in well-prepared but light, well-drained soil, Andrew was sure they would suffer from full exposure. To his

surprise, and my relief, they flourished. We are in some cases able to grow plants in the open in our temperate climate which in nature would normally be found in the shade. In their native home, the continental summer sun would be considerably hotter than here, so some shade is essential. Today these plants have retreated into scrubby places where they are safe from grazing animals and from man's scavenging of the land in order to grow crops. In most cases these are the only places where they have survived extinction.

As a beginner I did not realize that plants have their preferences and are adapted to special conditions. Let us take, for example, cultivated garden plants such as pyrethrums or double zinnias. These plants need what is generally termed 'good garden soil' and open sunny conditions. They have been developed and evolved from plants which originally liked and grew in open sunny places, so they cannot be expected to perform well in dim shady backyards where they would grow pale and leggy reaching for the light.

The majority of cultivars grown for their flowers could be planted in straight rows in the vegetable garden, where they have full sunlight and air all around them, and where they would provide good-quality flowers for picking. But there is an increasing interest among gardeners to use more plants as they are found growing in the wild, so you really do have to find out what the 'wild' is like. It is not enough to know that the plant came from China or Japan or America. Was it from the north, east, south or west? Was it from a hot, dry, gravelly slope or was it found in a soggy, boggy place? Many well-known herbaceous plants like rudbeckias, Michaelmas daisies and Golden Rod are mainly found in damp meadowlands of North America, while asphodels and many euphorbias are found in stony soil in countries around the Mediterranean which habitually have hot dry summers.

As far as plants grown mainly for their foliage are concerned, at the beginning of this century William Robinson was using many of them. They were grown in the gardens of the wealthy and the discerning, and slowly they spread into other gardens, but on the whole it was a small, charmed circle of cultivated people who travelled and mixed socially who knew of them. There were still many typical Victorian gardens full of salvias and other plants from the greenhouse put out in rows like guardsmen, but William Robinson and Gertrude Jekyll began the revolution towards a more natural style of planting. The writings of Vita Sackville-West carried it further, but the problem for many of their followers was where to find such plants. Most nurseries did not dare list plants with long Latin names.

Many wealthy people did not involve themselves in their gardens; they relied on their gardeners to do it all for them. Miss Ellen Willmott was an exception. She was a wealthy woman and a great gardener. She collected species plants and made a garden near Brentwood, in Essex, where she employed over 150 gardeners whom she trained herself with discipline and zeal. She brought from Switzerland a man of the mountains to create and tend her alpine garden, but I suspect few of her treasures percolated into the cottage gardens around.

After the Second World War, the situation changed. Many more people were seeking new interests after years of austerity. During the war we read and were enthralled by the inspired writing of Vita Sackville-West and of Margery Fish. At about that time I made the acquaintance of the late Sir Cedric Morris and his wonderful garden on the outskirts of Hadleigh in Suffolk. It was full of irises, poppies, tall verbascums, alliums and many other unusual plants which we grow in our gardens today, but which were rarely seen then. I think that for those of us who could visit his garden he became what Vita had been to the readers of her articles in the *Observer*. No doubt up and down the country there were people like them who were influencing a small circle of gardeners around them, which gradually grew and spread like yeast through all sections of society. Real gardeners see no class distinctions – dukes and dustmen are only too happy to talk together in a common language, the love of growing plants.

The idea of making a nursery of unusual plants came to me through my association with the Flower Club movement when it first began not long after the Second World War. Women were repressed and depressed after years of making do. They needed something to relieve the austerity of ration books, still in use five or six years after the end of the war because economically the country had not found its feet. They felt frustrated by shortages of materials. Suddenly flower arranging arrived, largely initiated by Constance Spry with her fresh and individual style. She, too, had the advantage of knowing Cedric Morris. She used to stay with him occasionally in Suffolk, and would go back to London with her car

Five years ago this piece of land was the remains of wasteland, covered with blackthorn and brambles on the upper level and black mud in the hollows. After draining it and adding truckloads of grit to open the close texture of the soil, it has become a valuable extension of our nursery stock beds. In the foreground kniphofias are seen with Hemerocallis *'Golden Chimes' behind them. I have interplanted the boundary line of oaks with young birch, willow, field maples and holly to break the west wind which blows unimpeded across the flat farm land beyond.*

full of flowers, seed-heads and wonderful leaves such as had never been seen in London flower shops before.

When I was about thirty years old, with two young children, Mrs Pamela Underwood, the founder of the Colchester Flower Club, came into my life. She was our neighbour in our first married home at Braiswick, Colchester, where we gardened alongside the ancient Roman ramparts on the outskirts of the town. Through the Flower Club, my eyes were opened to things I had never properly seen before, even though I thought I was an observant gardener. I became aware of plants in a new way, not only in the garden but on wasteland, on railway lines and on the salt marshes, foliage as well as flowers, even blackberry leaves. I stopped to pick them and see how pretty many are on the underside.

I discovered that it is possible to create an attractive design with many unexpected things. This was meat and drink to many women who had no gardens at all. They were being taught how to put together two or three leaves, a bud and a flower to make something attractive for their homes when previously they might not have bothered to make the attempt. They had thought that if they did not have a bunch of roses or gladioli, they had nothing to arrange.

At that time I was very fortunate because unlike many young women today who are obliged, even with young children, to go out to work, I was able to enjoy nearly twenty years of creative activities around the home which not only enriched my life at the time, but also proved to be helpful later on. I was much involved with the flower garden but I also ran the kitchen garden, and grew

This is a familiar sight in the nursery most evenings in summer when the automatic irrigation system is switched on section by section spraying a fine mist over the plants. Windy evenings are a problem so a back-up system of hand-held hoses is sometimes required to water areas that might still be dry.

unusual vegetables, encouraged by my old friend Sir Cedric. From him I obtained seeds of things like blue-podded beans (instead of the common scarlet runner beans), avocadello marrows, chicory, several kinds of radish, like 'China Rose' and 'Black Winter', and asparagus peas – all of which in those days, thirty-five years ago, were not to be found in seedsmen's catalogues.

At the same time I was bringing home from Sir Cedric's garden all kinds of seeds, cuttings and tiny scraps of this and that, and teaching myself about propagating unusual plants. This discipline was a good preparation for becoming a nurseryman.

The Nursery

I started the nursery with just one girl who had been working for my husband on the farm. By this time we had lived for about seven years in the new farmhouse we had built on the edge of wasteland between our neighbour's farm and ours, and the garden (which is the subject of the main chapters of this book) was taking shape. After a couple of years other women came along to help. Then when the farm was sold, Harry, the youngest man on the farm, came and joined me. He has now been with us, Andrew and I together, for 40 years.

The flower arranging movement transformed the nursery business in this country, as people like myself and Mary Pope, who started the first Flower Club in Dorchester, began to use more species plants. When I first started the nursery I would give demonstrations at flower clubs using only garden plants and that was my best publicity.

Mrs Pamela Underwood rang me one day and said, 'I want you to open a new flower club at Framlingham,' in Suffolk. I could not drive a car but I quickly learned, and just as quickly had to teach myself to do flower demonstrations. Before long I was doing them up and down the country, always taking flowers and foliage from the garden. The garden gave me confidence, although I knew the majority of demonstrators used florists' material. The response was astonishing. I, who had been growing these plants for fifteen years, had forgotten how unlikely it was that other people would know and grow euphorbias, hellebores and other green flowers with unusual foliage and textures. So the seed was sown in my mind that if I ever had the chance I would have a business one day and would call it 'Unusual Plants'.

Part of the nursery stock area, roped off from the sales area beyond. When plants are sold, fresh pots are stood out in the Sales area, ensuring that customers have good plants that have not been overhandled. Here also sufficient plants are reserved for postal customers to ensure as far as possible that they will not be disappointed. With a list of almost 2,000 different plants for sale, the propagating staff are busy throughout the year.

Today the nursery (now called 'The Beth Chatto Gardens') relies very much on the garden and the garden on the nursery. I could never have made the enterprise so large or so full of interesting plants without the money that comes from the nursery or the help of my dedicated staff. We need each other, and the visitors, too, make another contribution because they inspire me to make new plantings or redesign areas past their best. Gardens become elderly, just as we do, if we carry on doing the same things and fail to see them afresh. Although it is not my main intention to make a garden for the public, since I feel the appropriateness of the planting must come first, I am both inspired and sometimes chastised by comments I hear around me.

I look for sources of interesting plants all the time. Some people will occasionally say that we have so many plants here there cannot be any more we could want. Sometimes I feel there is not enough space for any more, but then I realize that all I have to do is renovate an area to create the space.

THE CHELSEA FLOWER SHOW

Over the last decade I have exhibited at The Chelsea Flower Show every year and it is through this world-famous show that many people have come to know me, my garden and my nursery.

Exhibiting there involves a great deal of hard work for both me and my staff. From February onwards I go round the nursery and the garden selecting plants, putting them in containers and then into protective tunnels. I have two types of tunnel – warm plastic ones (although they are not heated), so things are brought on more quickly than they would be outside, and green netting tunnels through which the rain can penetrate so they stay cool and moist. From Easter onwards I spend my time moving the plants I have selected from one tunnel to the other, like buns in an oven, bringing some on, and moving others into the cool to stop them flowering too soon.

Chelsea, unfortunately, comes at the busiest time of year for any nursery, when the staff are busy packing plants for mail order and the visitors start arriving in throngs. I personally prepare most of my plants for Chelsea, since I know exactly what I need and everyone else already has more than enough to do. I probably prepare about one thousand of them in order to have enough at the right stage of development when the great day arrives.

Two women gardeners are responsible for garden maintenance from May until the end of August. Weeds are not a serious problem because of the protective mulch of pulverized bark, but plants themselves sometimes become weeds if seeded in the wrong place where the mulch layer has worn thin. Others may encroach on their neighbours and need to be restricted. From September until the end of April staff are busy packing plant orders, but during mid-winter time is usually found to cut down and tidy the gardens for the last time before the new spring growth commences.

Part of my exhibit at Chelsea, 1987, showing overall, and within the design, the asymmetrical triangle on which I base many of my planting schemes. Smaller verticals such as the Verbascum *and* Sisyrinchium *help to create smaller triangles – that is, groups which form a satisfying shape together – within the whole design. The large-leaved plants of* Verbascum pulverulentum *are creating focal points, acting as full-stops among small-scale plants that could look fussy by themselves.*

My Chelsea display is based on the same theme every year, echoing the theme of the garden. I have an area to fill with plants that looks, when empty, as big as a tennis court. In fact it is only about 6 × 9 m/20 × 30 ft, but it still seems enormous when it has to be transformed with plants. I go to London with the lorries on the Thursday before the show opens five days later and I check to see who is showing alongside me, so that I can organize the stand to best effect. Just as with my gardening, I have to make decisions on the spot. I cannot make plans on paper. I only know in my mind that I will have a damp area, with plants for cool conditions, a dry shady side and at the opposite side a group of plants for hot dry gardens. To that end I collect plants to form varied groups.

I do not aim for a showy display of unseasonal plants in flower but tend to concentrate on the effect of contrasting shapes, sizes and designs of leaves. I hope that people will notice them, maybe for the first time. I not only use spectacular leaves like those of rheums, gunneras and hostas but also others from the dry garden, like santolinas, blue rues, ballotas and salvias.

So far, to my delight, our efforts have met with great success: ten gold medals in succession.

Principles of Planting

Anthemis tinctoria 'E.C. Buxton' is one of my favourite plants. Soft creamy-yellow daisies appear continuously from midsummer until late autumn.

MANY GARDENERS are full of enthusiasm, but at the same time are often very conscious that they are not getting their planting right, and that they need some guidelines. Perhaps they are dissatisfied with the effect they create – for some reason, the plants do not look well together. Often they have very little idea of plant grouping, and dot plants around the garden like pins in a pincushion; where there is a space, they put in the latest acquisition without even stopping to think whether it is the sunny or the shady side of the garden and whether this matters or not.

I was recently asked to write an article on planting for problem situations by a journalist who felt other readers might value advice on where and how to plant. She herself was having trouble with the planting in the sunny part of her garden. Curiously enough, she was doing quite well with the shady cool side, which she had realized could look very attractive, but on the hot dry side the plants were dying. She was probably planting things like hostas, primulas or gentians, plants not adapted to such conditions. In most gardens the design effect depends on flowers rather than foliage. Once flowering is over, the plants either stand there looking bedraggled because the conditions are too dry or they are cut down, leaving a gap in the planting. In either case, the garden may end up looking characterless and ragged. The disastrous results make you think you have a 'problem' situation when all you have is a site that different species of plants would enjoy.

Perhaps one of the reasons why people sometimes make mistakes is that they fail to work from the right end of the equation. Instead of accepting that what they have is a sunny site, working out what will grow on it and making the most of that, they collect ideas about plants from books. Inspired by beautiful pictures of blue this and yellow that, they then go to the garden centre and buy plants they cannot resist, thinking that all the plants require is

When we began our garden this area was part of a boggy meadow where cows sank up to their knees (or whatever those parts of a cow are called). After several false starts, caused mainly by inadequate preparation of such a difficult site, I was finally able to plant this group. The Marsh Spurge (Euphorbia palustris) and the Ostrich Plume Fern (Matteuccia struthiopteris) both love damp soil while the large-leaved Lysichitum americanum has its roots deep down beneath shallow water on the edge of the pond. Pink pokers of Polygonum bistorta 'Superbum' add soft colour to many shades of spring green, while the bold round leaves of Ligularia 'Gregynog Gold' and short blue spires of Ajuga reptans take care of the foreground.

to be put into the earth. It does not occur to them that the plant may not like the situation. Even when they are not seduced by flower colour but commendably look for good foliage form, they may be no more successful. If you have a hot sunny garden and plant ferns or hostas or other plants with delicate foliage that scorches in the sun, the effect will be depressing because the leaves will be damaged. There are plenty of colourful annuals like French Marigolds and Larkspur which will grow in that hot dry soil, provided you water them in and go on watering them, but there is then no background to the planting. All you have is hot garish colours and the garden lacks what I call the 'furniture' – the permanent planting. I feel that the garden should be attractive as far as possible all the year round. It is easiest to do this in a hot dry garden with many of the grey-leaved plants and those with tough leathery leaves which will last through the winter. Although in this part of the world it can be very cold indeed in winter and the ground may occasionally freeze up to a depth of about 45cm/18in, many Mediterranean-type plants will usually survive in well-drained gravel.

ATTITUDES TO PLANTING

The art of gardening has changed considerably over the centuries. In the seventeenth century garden designers like André le Nôtre (who made the great garden at Versailles for Louis XIV) were pushing nature back, sweeping the forest away from the great, stately châteaux. In those days, this had a practical reason: the forest was still full of wolves and bears, and so there had to be a barrier of walls and hedges around the garden. Everything else in the garden was formal, too – long stretches of water echoed the straight lines of the boundary fences and edging. There were none of the wild grasses and foliage plants that we enjoy using today. On the contrary, almost everything was clipped and manicured into formal shapes and designs. It was an age when gentlemen paraded up and down between geometrically designed parterres. They needed to feel safe and civilized; nature was not something to be enjoyed but something to be tamed or kept at bay.

Nowadays we are trying hard to return to nature, perhaps because we are overcivilized. Also many people travel and have the opportunity to see plants growing in their natural habitat. Some may feel the urge to try to cultivate these plants seen

Beyond this north-facing bank of clay there was originally a group of tall elms which gave protection and a natural grandeur to this part of the garden. But elm disease destroyed them and we were left with a wide open sky. Among the trees planted to fill the gap was this tall silver-leaved willow, Salix alba. *Beneath it, enjoying partial shade, grow the purple-leaved elder* Sambucus nigra 'Purpurea' *and the yellow variegated form of* Acer negundo, A.n. 'Elegans'. *Below them grows the American woodland plant,* Smilacina racemosa, *while* Hosta sieboldiana 'Elegans' *creates the focal point with large calming blue leaves.*

growing in the wild to bring something of the peace and tranquillity of nature into their gardens.

Many gardeners are not aware that the most well known garden plants have been developed by hybridization and selection from plants found growing in the wild. They tend to think of them as products of the horticulturists. We do not, after all, go out and pick carrots from the hedge; we have tamed vegetables and made them palatable for human use. So man has made ornamental plants for the garden proper for his use, and ideas of what is proper have changed from generation to generation. The mop-headed chrysanthemums, huge dahlias and statuesque gladioli so popular with generations of plant breeders are, after all, only cultivated and 'improved' forms of plants that all originated in the wild somewhere, in a much simpler form.

When they begin gardening, many people, particularly city-dwellers, are often almost totally ignorant of nature. They think of wild flowers as weeds like dandelions and bindweed. If you have not learned much botany at school, the plants that grow wild and the plants that grow in garden centres seem poles apart.

THE INFLUENCE OF CLIMATE

It would be wrong to frighten people off by suggesting there is a mystique about planting, that you must put plants in exactly the right situation. Many of them will tolerate quite a wide range of conditions, but certainly when you come to using species plants you cannot go too far beyond their natural range. Take, for example, rhododendrons which come from mountainous areas throughout Asia and Northern America. They receive ample rainfall and although they are growing at high altitudes where the power of the sun will be great, the constant accumulation of clouds will also keep their foliage moist. If you try to grow rhododendrons in the drier parts of the British Isles, the leaves will scorch and wither. The same is true of azaleas. These are under-storey plants – that is, they are found growing in the shade of woodland trees. Many of them are from Japan, and again the Japanese islands are affected by moisture-laden air. They have a climate more like the south-west peninsula of Devon and Cornwall. (Incidentally both azaleas and rhododendrons are adapted to acid peaty conditions and will not tolerate chalky soil.)

The hardiness of plants is conditioned by the type of soil you have because this exaggerates or counteracts the climatic condi-tions. Poor sandy or gravelly soil is warmer in winter because it is not full of icy water. In summer the plants grow tough and wiry in such soils. If they were in better soil they would grow soft and sappy and would collapse in the first frost. When I first came here I planted cistuses in some of my more retentive soil. They grew wonderfully well, but I lost them in a hard winter. Heathers, on the other hand, do not like the driest of conditions. They grow on moors – a very different habitat from East Anglian gravel. Heathers from Dartmoor or Scotland will not do on a soil with very low rainfall. But on certain East Anglian sandy soils Ling and Bell Heather form a peat layer and thus do survive and create heathland.

I am writing and gardening to help people grow plants in the climate and conditions that exist for them. To pour water on the garden in times of drought is now almost impossible: as soon as there is a drought, watering in gardens is usually banned to keep the reserves of water for the population and the food crops. Provided you choose your plants carefully, you do not need to go in for regular watering. I certainly do not subscribe to it.

If you do as much as you can to improve the soil texture before planting, and protect it with mulches like bark and peat (or even less attractive but equally useful ones like old carpets, straw, paper, black polythene) until the plants can become established, you will help the garden to mature more quickly. At the end of the first season the plants themselves will already cover much of the ground. If you lift a plant even in dry weather, there will always be some moisture under it. But even mulching will not get you very far if you do not use plants that are adapted to drought.

If you have energy, time and enthusiasm you can always improve the conditions in the garden to enable you to grow a wider range of plants. Most of us, however, have to live, more or less, with what we have. In my first married home, on the outskirts of Colchester, I had a garden on chalky boulder clay which, when it

As far as possible I try to cover the surface of my soil with foliage. It is nature's way of protecting the structure from battering by rain or from capping when it is exposed to wind and sun. Before the plants have had time to spread themselves I cover the earth between them with a mulch. I use pulverized bark, but peat, spent hops or any weed-free material that is not unsightly and will rot down eventually would do. We try to disturb the mulch as little as possible as any nodule of soil exposed will produce an unwanted weed. A layer, about 5cm/2in thick, stifles most weed seedlings before they can reach the light. The weeding is now a pleasure in comparison with the work we had to do when weeds re-seeded as thick as the hairs on a cat's back. The mound of yellow in this picture is a Japanese grass, Hakonechloa macra *'Albo- aurea'.*

dried out, set hard. There was no way I could grow bog-loving plants, yet when offered wonderful plants like *Astilbe* and *Lysichitum* I thought, in my youth and ignorance, that I could grow them. I tried and I lost them. No matter how much compost I put into the soil, those plants could not exist with such low rainfall, their distress aggravated by drying winds.

SOIL

Many gardening books discuss endlessly the acidity and alkalinity of the soil but fail to talk about its texture. For some plants, like the azaleas and rhododendrons I mentioned, the acidity or alkalinity of the soil is important – but there are only a few. People who live on chalky soil and want to grow acid-loving plants have to add certain chemicals to the soil to neutralize it, but this has to be a continuing process, since rain will wash the chemicals out, and more dissolved chalk will upset the balance. I prefer not to try and instead choose plants that suit the conditions. But you can grow far far more plants if you do something about the texture of the soil – and you can forget about whether it is acid or chalk. You just need to find out which plants are lime-haters and avoid them, if you have calcareous soil, or if you have very acid, peaty soil, add chalk.

It is the *texture* of the soil – the blend of air, drainage and nutrients – that really matters. You have three basic soil types – sand and gravel, silt, and clay. If you hold it in your hand, light gravel or sandy soil will probably fall apart, even when wet, and when dry it runs through your fingers like sand in an egg-timer. In long periods of drought these types of soil are disastrous for many plants as they simply dry out. Obviously they drain only too well, and what you need is some kind of moisture-retaining material like peat, or better still, humus – which also adds nutrients to the soil. Mulching the surface after planting also helps to prevent excess evaporation. Once you have improved a light soil so it will hold together you can grow a wider range of plants. Many of my woodland plants – hostas, pulmonarias and cranesbills – are growing in the same kind of soil as my drought-loving plants just a few yards away, but the shade from a huge oak and holly protects the woodland plants for much of the day when the little Mediterranean garden lies in full sun.

On the lower side of the oak-holly bed we have a different soil, poor and fine-textured, which is a dense silt. To this you need to add a lot of grit, for although it has good water-holding properties, plants with fine roots cannot push their way through it when it becomes compacted. What it needs is a generous application of grit to the top spit, otherwise it will not breathe. I also use bonfire waste, which is gritty, to open the texture.

In areas of heavy clay – the most difficult soil to improve – you have to wait until the soil is in a manageable state. If it has dried as hard as concrete or has become as wet as butter, you cannot handle it. Ideally you need to dig it in the autumn to allow the frost to break it up, and then dig in plenty of grit and humus in the spring. If you live in an area that has solid clay from one end of the county to the other and cannot lay your hands on gravelly soil to mix with it, you will have to come to terms with it and concentrate on those plants with penetrating roots. Gardeners on very light soils will be envious of clay's water-retention and feel equally frustrated.

People sometimes ask me how often they should try to tackle the job of improving their soil. Obviously you are not going to do this every year to an established bed, but every six or seven years I remove plants from part of a border, divide the ones that have become overgrown and rejuvenate the bed – both the soil and the planting. I take the herbaceous plants out and leave in the ones that hate being moved (the ones with very deep roots which, in any

These two pictures, taken with a year's interval between, are of different aspects of the small shade garden below a large oak and holly that I have re-made over the past two or three years. The area is also shaded by a large tree, Paulownia imperialis, free-standing in the wide grass walk beyond. The picture below showed me an obvious fault as photographs often do. Originally we did not put down the 'stepping stones' of wooden blocks, surrounded by crushed bark, and the narrow edging of tiles used to define the edge of the bed was not offensive, especially when mat-forming plants crept over to soften it, but some were far too successful and had to be removed.

The second picture looks much better without the hard line of tiles. It is taken from the opposite direction showing how the eye is gently led out of the shade across the mown grass to another border whose shape and colour scheme harmonize with the plants on either side of this curving 'woodland' walk. Another season and the view will have changed again. Some plants will have filled in spaces as I had hoped they would; others may have died. (Why? we must ask ourselves.) Others again will have misbehaved and will have to be replanted where they cannot destroy their neighbours. No scene is ever quite the same from one year to the next.

The Giant Hogweed (Heracleum mantegazzianum)
*stands isolated and majestic
on the edge of a small copse
where I have recently started
to naturalize snowdrops,
dwarf narcissi and other suitable plants. Its noble stature,
huge carved leaves and great
wheel-shaped heads of flowers
create a landscape effect in
long grass, which will be cut
when the bulbs have com-
pletely died down. Care must
be taken with the Giant Hogweed – the sap is toxic and
can cause severe blistering of
the skin. It is* not *a plant to
put where children may play
beneath it.*

case, can cope with the soil). I dig the soil to at least a spit deep and
put in whatever it happens to need – grit, compost or well-rotted
farm manure. Minor renovation of a small planting area can pay too
– you do not have to dig up a whole border.

DESIGNING

Two influences have helped me in design. First has been my
husband, with his studies of plant ecology teaching that plants
prefer to be in an environment similar to the one they have in the
wild, so you do not simply jumble plants up according to whim.
Secondly, when I was involved in the flower arranging movement
(which I talked about in the introduction, on page 14) I made
friends with an old lady whose husband had connections with
Japan. She had a great many books on flower arranging in Japan,
and I studied them with great interest. You cannot translate the
arrangements directly into western-style houses, as they do not
suit our style and tastes in furniture, but looking at them I began to
appreciate the golden principle of design – the asymmetrical
triangle between earth, man and heaven – which is so beautiful
and gives such a wonderful feeling of balance. The art is in making

everything flow together in harmony. Although my garden is in no way Japanese, because I could not make one in this landscape even if I wanted to, I have assimilated some of their principles and ideas. I hope overall there is a balance and a harmony of shape, form, outline and texture. I never realized at the time that these principles would have such a profound and long-lasting influence, but they do underpin all my ideas about planting. Take my Mediterranean Garden, which is full of many different types of plant, but which (I hope) no one would find garish or bitty. Why not? Because the plants are all adapted to much the same conditions. They blend well together while any monotony arising from so many small-leaved plants is broken by the use of handsome architectural ones like Cardoon and tall imposing fountains of grass like *Stipa gigantea*.

'Harmonious' is a word I would like to apply to the garden, meaning that overall there is a feeling of simplicity and harmony, with wide grass curves and gentle walkways. I hope there is nothing abrupt or startling. I always prefer to plant in groups, and leave spaces in between the groups so that the design has greater depth, and provides glimpses of different areas of the garden beyond. Big full-stop plants punctuate the design and add contrast, but never in a way that shocks or startles. Surprise elements are necessary; shock tactics are not.

PLANNING FOR COLOUR

Although I have views on which colours go well together in the garden (I mention some of them on page 94), I would never deliberately plan a white garden for instance. If you do, the danger is that you are going to take white plants requiring very different conditions and try to grow them all in one area. That goes against my theories of gardening. A white polygonum needing moisture and heavy clay is not going to perform well if it is planted in the dry soil that suits *Gaura lindheimeri* and white-flowered *Dianthus*. In my opinion, they just do not go together and I would be surprised if they all survived the same conditions.

I am not drawn to a garden planned in this way, I find it artificial. It is heresy to say so, but the White Garden at Sissinghurst is not something I can totally admire. I first saw it many years ago and although my impression of it then was that it was very romantic, seeing it again recently I am not sure that I liked it, and I certainly

Most visitors gasp with admiration when Camellia *'Donation' is in full flower, but it is the combination of shapes and textures that gives me the most pleasure all the year round. This is an example of what I call 'painting the sky'. It is easy enough to lay colour on the ground with annuals or herbaceous plants, but we need encouragement to look up to the sky in winter as well as in summer. The combination of deciduous trees and conifers adds an open screen as well as evergreen protection, making me feel secure without being oppressed.*

did not feel at home in it even though I was very interested in the individual plants and excited by the great variety of white-flowering ones.

Although I know that they are an integral part of classically styled gardens, I am not keen on clipped box hedges forming a barrier between me and the plants they enclose. I prefer plants to merge and flow together to soften the edges of the paths. When I say I do not like box hedges, it does not mean that I cannot accept them somewhere else, in the same way that one can enjoy many different styles of painting.

Take a garden like Hidcote. Although I admire the combination of colours, the planting and design, with the compartments of the garden spread like rooms with Persian carpets of plants, I would never choose to make a garden like that.

Here I am never concerned if the colour has gone out of a border. I would not rush in to remedy the lack with begonias and dahlias. My style of gardening does not depend too much on colour and, where it does, it is in a more subtle way. Throughout spring and summer waves of soft colour ebb and flow through the basic patterns of foliage plants, which all produce flowers in their turn. Then, as the season wanes, little jewel-like autumn flowers add sparkle. A feeling for shape is just as important as a sense of colour. Often people who use colour very well do not pay attention to form and outline.

When thinking of colour schemes for planting, you must again consider the situation. Where you have overcast skies, soft light most of the time and green that almost hurts because it is so bright, then I think that the really savage reds, purples and blues of certain cultivars do not look right. Against stonework they look fine, but in most temperate gardens the softer colours and smaller flowers of the species plants blend more sympathetically with the green environment.

The flowers of shade-loving plants are less brightly coloured on the whole than those of sun-loving ones. You are not going to get brilliant scarlet flowers on a shade-loving plant – they tend to be more pastel-coloured on the whole. Many of the really brightly coloured flowers come from the desert areas of the world, where you have a dark blue sky and a coppery sun bearing down. If you used pale colours in such a situation they would look washed out, but the combination of brown or red soil with the scarlets, yellows

This scene in midsummer is part of one of the open borders on retentive soil. In the foreground is Hosta ventricosa 'Variegata', *the colour of whose edges is repeated in the creamy-white flowers of* Filipendula palmata 'Alba'. *The yellow saucers of* Hypericum 'Hidcote' *harmonize with the young new growths of a* Chamaecyparis. *I would like to divide and spread the pale yellow* Hemerocallis *which looks isolated in the background.*

and bright purples of big, brash flowers can be dramatic. I find it difficult to use some strong flower colours. However, if I use them in small groups, and if the flowers themselves are not huge, they can be successful, like *Crocosmia* 'Lucifer', which I am just finding out how to place. I cannot mix it with my grey planting, which tends to have a lot of mauves and pinks and pale colours. But elsewhere I have found a way of combining it with acid yellows and the dark blues of salvias, which balance its intensity.

You can use intense colours, but preferably in small amounts. Too large a group of strongly coloured plants can be offputting. They are best used as an accent, preferably with paler shades of the same colour grouped around them. You need to avoid a series of plants fighting each other in blocks of primary colours. Two strong shades together virtually cancel each other out, as your eye does not know where to turn. Each flower colour should enhance those nearby, either by blending in tone or by providing subtle contrast. If you use it in this way, it enables you to see the other colours better. If they are all there in the same degree, the impact is so much less. Although it pays to lead in gradually to stronger colours, there are exceptions to the rule. I think the big blocks of guardsman-like rows of vividly coloured tulips in our public parks look wonderful, but you do need to be careful when using colour to observe its intensity, as it can be overpowering in a small garden.

PLANNING FOR SMALL GARDENS

If my garden were smaller I would have to think differently about the planting. In small gardens it is particularly important that you choose plants that offer more than just attractive flowers. At the risk of becoming a bore on the subject (it is a topic I keep returning to, both in this book and in others), I think all the plants in the garden, and even more so in a small garden, must have interesting or valuable leaf texture, colour or form.

I think the same principles of planting for foliage first apply there too. You can have colour, but not *sheets* of colour, in small gardens. You have to give up the idea of great drifts of primulas, you may not even have roses (apart from one or two climbing or specimen roses), and you certainly will not be planting in clumps of fives or tens. If on the other hand the garden is completely overshadowed by tall buildings or trees, you can grow only the shade-loving plants which gives your planting natural harmony.

In a very small garden your aim has to be to cover every available surface with leaves that harmonize with one another. On the sunny side you will have the drought-loving varieties with grey, succulent or leathery leaves, and on the shady side you will have ferns, hostas, dicentras – the more delicate-foliaged plants.

A tiny garden can have special interest and if your garden is very small-scale, you can devote much more time to grooming your plants. You will probably need to because they are all so much more visible. You also have to make sure that they do not rush all over one another. Some will probably have to be removed when you realize their habits do not suit such a tiny garden, because they are too invasive – ajugas are an obvious example.

There is hardly a garden that does not have two different climates, created by the shade of house walls. When a garden is in full sun most of the day, you can add shade by planting suitable trees and shrubs. (You can also create new environments for smaller plants by making raised beds.)

If you have a new house on a housing estate you probably will not have any shade except under the walls – perhaps a boundary wall, or beneath the north- or east-facing walls of the house. If the road runs east to west, which side of the street you live on is important –

This is part of a raised bed beneath a warm south-west-facing wall. It reminds me of visits I made to old ladies when I was a child, and being shown collections of precious miniatures – pieces of silver, jade or ceramics – arranged in glass-topped cabinets. Now probably the same age as those 'old ladies', I have no glass-topped cabinets, but plants have become my *treasures, whether rare or two-a-penny. I delight in arranging them and never tire of looking at them, whether they are in flower or not. The plants include various sizes and colours of* Sempervivum, Sedum acre *full of yellow stars and* Raoulia hookeri *running like quicksilver among them. Rosettes of* Primula auricula, *a form with white-powdered leaves (and beige-pink flowers in spring), add a bolder accent in the top of the picture.*

gardens on one side will all be south-facing and those on the other side of the street will all be north-facing. The sunny side of the street which gets the hot afternoon sun will be able to grow very different plants from those on the north, cool side of the street. The north-facing back gardens will provide ideal homes for hostas and hydrangeas, while the houses on the other side of the street will be able to grow these in their front gardens, and vice versa.

I know intimately three small gardens that belong to members of my family which I see from time to time. My two daughters and my twin brother each have small town gardens with raised beds and they have exploited both the sunny and shady sides of their gardens. Although the girls did not seem very interested in gardening when they were young – in those days, as far as they were concerned, mother's garden was a muddy field full of sticks – they must have taken in more than I realized because they have certainly been imaginative in creating their own gardens. By making raised beds you seem to give yourself more room in the garden. My daughters' raised beds are gently and irregularly curving, enclosing a sitting area, but straight edges might be preferred in some situations. It helps if you plant the beds so that mats of plants like *Helianthemum* spill over the edges to soften the hard lines. But the keynote is simplicity, otherwise the design can look very cluttered.

Here is a picture to inspire designers of fabric or embroidery, picked out by the mind and eye of the photographer. As a portrait of the plants themselves it could be faulted, but how easy it is to do that and fail to see a different dimension. Although we cannot tell if the plants are 90cm/3ft tall or a few inches above ground level, it does not matter if you are enjoying the design of soft colours and starkly contrasting shapes. But to ease your curiosity, the prickly rosettes looking as if cut out of silvery-blue metal are Eryngium giganteum, *better known as Miss Willmott's Ghost and 75cm/2½ft tall. (Miss Willmott used to scatter the seed from her pocket as she walked in other people's gardens.) Next to it are the creamy-yellow 45cm-/1½ft-high heads of* Achillea taygetea, *while self-sown among them, making the perfect colour harmony, is a 1m-/3ft-tall apricot form of the Peruvian lily,* Alstroemeria ligtu.

You certainly do not want to waste space with grass because it becomes threadbare with wear and if you are a busy city-dweller you will not want the work involved. My brother cannot now manage to mow a lawn and so has paved the centre of his garden instead. The long, narrow, sloping site has been terraced as well, and the areas of paving are quite small, with the retaining walls inset here and there to take a seat. The terraces help to break up the straight lines of the paving, which has the added advantage that it can be easily swept and tidied. At the far end of the garden where there is a tool shed and compost heap, the path is gravelled, making a pleasant contrast of texture. I am not a great one for dabbing little plants in among paving, although it can be done if you are prepared to look after them, and provided you take care that the planting does not look spotty and messy.

Another solution for a town garden is to use water to create a very different atmosphere. Even the smallest pools can bring an extra dimension to the garden setting. Being able to touch water, watch reflections, or sit in the shade of arching bamboos (provided their roots are restricted) will blot out the bricks and mortar beyond by concentrating the mind in a tiny oasis of green.

THINKING AHEAD

Gardeners rarely become bored, but even the most enthusiastic of us become exhausted from time to time – not just physically, but emotionally and mentally as well. We get frustrated, as does everyone else, by the weather, or pests, or whatever problem may be paramount. No one can live on a top-note all the time. If I am downcast about something or other, a walk round the garden almost any day of the year will usually restore me. I must confess that after the freak hurricane in October 1987 there were times on gloomy November mornings when I did not want to go into the garden at all. But once I pulled myself together and started thinking about the tasks ahead – of how I would actually tackle the damage from both the storms and the unusually wet summer, the enthusiasm started to come back. I believe it is working in and re-making the garden that gives the most enjoyment, far more than simply admiring the results. It can well be the digging and delving on a miserable winter's day that starts to lift your spirits, and then suddenly you may see a way to make something fresh, to bring new vitality into the garden.

Hostas can come forward to highlight a scene in late autumn with glowing shades of honey and amber, provided they have not been ruined by slug damage or, as here, burnt by salt (in this case, when the freak hurricane of October '87 swept up out of the English Channel and caused unimaginable havoc over south-east England). Apart from the loss of trees and shrubs, foliage was withered by the salt-laden winds.

The Entrance Garden

Sedum spectabile 'Brilliant' quickly makes large clumps of fleshy grey-green leaves, good to look at all season, and finally produces, in September, large flat heads of vivid-pink flowers, very attractive to butterflies. In the same bed Sedum 'Autumn Joy', with brick-red starry flowers, will be ignored by butterflies, but covered with honey bees.

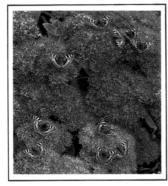

This planting shows a curious combination of both dry- and damp-loving plants in this long entrance border. The soil in my garden can vary within a couple of paces and here, I think, a spring, travelling beneath the field beyond the hedge, must be sufficiently near the surface to keep the soil damp, since some of the plants, such as the mauve and white fluffy-headed Thalictrum aquilegiifolium, *would not stand a dry summer in gravel soil. The plants were introduced from seed in the compost we used to improve the bed. The tall mulleins,* Verbascum pulverulentum, *and the broad-leaved* Artemisia × latiloba 'Valerie Finnis', *do not seem to suffer from wet feet, so presumably they are in a drier piece of soil.*

WHEN YOU COME in through the main gate, the first impression is of the great sweep of the west-facing border on your left-hand side. Originally I had intended to put in only shrubs here, and began by planting deciduous trees at the back of the border as a windbreak with laurels, hollies and cotoneasters to form groups of drought-resisting evergreens. A few years later I planted the hedge of × *Cupressocyparis leylandii* behind as extra protection. Now the border is very mixed, with trees, shrubs, perennials and bulbs, as the wider the contrast of shapes and forms the better it looks.

I consider the planting of this very large border to be 'coarse' planting as opposed to the type of planting in my little Mediterranean Garden behind the house (see page 128) where the groups are smaller in scale and the plants themselves are smaller. This is a big entrance garden, deliberately planned to be low-maintenance because we do not have the time to spend on a border far away from the rest of the garden. Rather than fussy planting with hundreds of varieties, I initially put in large groups of a few varieties of bold and easy plants, like bergenias and achilleas. Over the years these groups have extended themselves. After a few years I decided to make it more interesting because I feel that even in a garden this size every little bit is important, and when I am looking for space for new plants I can reduce some of these large masses and make room for smaller groups of different plants. The border itself is long (over 300m/320yd) and quite wide (about 6m/20ft), and as you drive along it on the way to park your car you see the large-scale effects of form. People used to drive past it without giving it much attention but since I put in more individually worthwhile plants, they are drawn to walk across the mown grass to view it. Although I have concentrated on creating contrast in leaf form, the planting is not without colour. On a sunny day in winter the big glistening

Bergenia leaves showing many tones of red make exciting contrast with other evergreens.

Bergenias need the right setting. I use them as major 'full-stop' plants among small-leaved foliage plants. Their big round leathery leaves catching the light in the sun are a marvellous accent and foil to the crinkly fussy leaves of *Cistus*, *Santolina* and Spanish Gorse (*Genista hispanica*). They look lovely, too, against the vertical lines of *Iris foetidissima*, with its striking strap-shaped leaves, and they all provide different tones and colours – especially in winter when many leaves are reddened by cold. The hebe nearby makes a lovely contrast of scale and texture. People often seem surprised that I make so much use of bergenias, but I think they have seen them looking sad and flabby among small bedding plants, whereas they need the contrast of other striking plant forms to show off their handsome leaves.

Quite often people fail to be bold enough in their plant groupings, and then do not get the full effect. Of course, if you have a very small garden and you love collecting plants it is tempting to try and put as many in as you can, but one plant alone rarely looks good. One clump of *Iris foetidissima* can be very effective, but you need at least three plants of *Bergenia* to form a bold clump. Again, if bergenias are left year after year they become leggy, with long woody stems. It is better to dig them up and divide and replant them every few years.

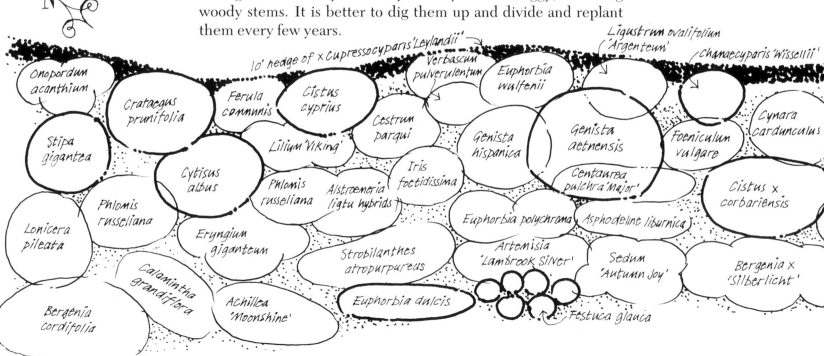

The way you group plants together is the whole essence of gardening. There are many ways of doing this, which is just as it should be – it would be very dull if everybody put their plants together in the same way. Designing a garden is rather like painting. Two painters will take the same pigments and will produce an entirely different picture, just as we do with our plants.

But there are some rules. In this border we have an example of the importance of choosing plants that are appropriate for the site. The soil here is very poor – the same dry gravel that I have in the Mediterranean Garden. Over the years I have added humus and a mulch of straw at the back of the borders, which is helping to feed the soil and improve the texture. But it is a free-draining gravel and if we have a drought in summer then these plants may have no measurable water from June till September. They have all been chosen because they can withstand these conditions – with leathery leaves (like bergenias), or finely cut leaves (like santolinas), or 'fat' leaves (like sedums) to help them retain moisture. Although they may suffer in times of prolonged drought, they will not die and this is the main consideration behind my choice of plants – here you will see no asters, golden rods, hostas or delphiniums, all of which need retentive soil and adequate rainfall.

The border is backed now, as I said, by a × *Cupressocyparis leylandii* hedge. I always swore I would not have any more hedges to cut but we had to have a boundary between us and our neighbour's fruit farm. We also needed something to keep out the north-east winds, which sweep straight across the North Sea from the Russian Steppes. Now about 3m/10ft high and not much more than 45cm/18in through, it makes a good, protective background.

For small gardens there are slow-growing hedging plants on a more compact scale that would be preferable, but I chose Leylandii because I have plenty of land (actually, no one ever has *plenty* of land, because once you become besotted with plants you want every bit). This hedge forms the nearest approach I have to an architectural wall and it makes a simple background to the big bold border. It continues through the nursery and is very acceptable there too. I thought about it carefully before I decided to plant it. Whether the woodland strip I had considered making and planting with trees and shrubs all along the boundary would have been a better windbreak – or even as good – is, I think, arguable. Maintaining it would have been just as much of a problem,

Part of the south-west-facing entrance border

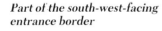

onicera ...ggesens 'gold'

Crambe cordifolia

Euphorbia wulfenii

Salvia officinalis 'Purpurascens'

Artemisia × latifolia

Crambe maritima

Phuopsis stylosa

Bergenia cordifolia

Artemisia absinthium 'Lambrook Silver'

Onopordum acanthium

BERGENIA

These are among the most valuable plants for ground cover. Being evergreen, they are always a feature. Most people only know the commonly grown form *B . × schmidtii* and are prepared to dismiss all others although this is the least attractive bergenia, never changing colour in winter and remaining leaden-green. In the design of the garden, well placed groups of bergenias often make a focal point to a border or have a calming effect among many smaller, more fussy leaves. Many of them also provide rich winter foliage colour.

B. cordifolia
Has large rounded leaves with crinkled edges and large, showy, soft-pink flower heads. 45cm/1½ft. Zone 4.

B. cordifolia 'Purpurea'
A superb plant with large rounded wavy leaves, ideal for ground cover. Occasionally in summer odd leaves dying off turn bright red or yellow while winter frost burnishes them all to purplish-red. The flower-stalks, the colour and thickness of rhubarb, support dangling sprays of vivid magenta flowers intermittently throughout summer. 45–60cm/1½–2ft. Zone 4.

B. crassifolia
Has smaller leaves than B. cordifolia. They are fresh-green in summer, flat and spoon-shaped, and held upright in rosettes so that the richly carmine backs contrast with the polished green and bronze fronts in autumn. In May soft-pink flowers make a fine display. 38cm/15in. Zone 4.

HYBRIDS

B. × 'Abendglut'
Neat rosettes of crinkly-edged rounded leaves turn rich maroon and plum-red in winter. Semi-double vivid rose-red flowers are produced in spring. 30cm/1ft. Zone 6.

B. × 'Admiral'
The leaves are valued for their bronze and crimson tints in winter and are erect, oval and weather-resistant. In spring, cherry-pink flowers are held on stems well above them. 30cm/1ft. Zone 6.

B. × 'Ballawley'
Largest of all with shining fresh-green leaves all summer, bronzed and reddened by frost. It has branching heads of rose-red flowers on tall stems in spring, a few still appearing in the autumn. 60cm/2ft. Zone 6.

B. × 'Beethoven'
Large dense clusters of white flowers flushing pink as they mature are held in coral-red calyces in April. 30cm/1ft. Zone 6.

B. × 'Eric Smith'
This superb Bergenia is the best for winter effect. Its large, rounded, crinkled leaves have polished bronze-tinted surfaces whose backs glow rich carmine-red. 45cm/1½ft. Zone 6.

B. × 'Morgenrote' ('Morning Blush')
Large rosettes of rounded leaves produce dense heads of cherry-pink flowers in spring and often an impressive second flowering later in the summer. 45cm/1½ft. Zone 6.

B. × 'Silberlicht' ('Silver Light')
In late spring this has large striking trusses of pure-white flowers which flush pink with age or from weather conditions. 30cm/1ft. Zone 6.

B. × 'Sunningdale'
Vivid rose-pink flowers are held on bright coral stems. The foliage has good autumn and winter colour. 30–38cm/12–15in. Zone 6.

B. × 'Sunningdale'

B. × 'Admiral'

B. × 'Silberlicht'

B. × 'Abendglut'

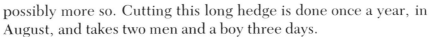
possibly more so. Cutting this long hedge is done once a year, in August, and takes two men and a boy three days.

As part of my effort to introduce more variety into the border I planted *Ipheion uniflorum* whose light blue flowers appear early in spring, grouped among dark blue hyacinths for contrast. The cultivated hyacinths may seem out of character, but over many years I have added them, in shades of pink, blue and white, to odd corners of the open sunny borders where they flower early and provide scent and colour to pick for the house. They lose that over-developed look they have when prepared for forcing bowls – their offsets produce more slender spikes of flowers.

Tall stands of the Crown Imperial Fritillary (*Fritillaria imperialis*) shoot up rapidly in April, while the taller alliums, *Allium aflatunense* and *A. bulgaricum*, make interesting verticals in May and June. Large bulky masses of *Euphorbia wulfenii* and the lower-growing *E. polychroma* illuminate the border for months, from March until June, with vivid lime-green heads. Woven through many green-leaved plants including oriental poppies, spurges and bergenias are grey and silver mounds of *Ballota*, *Santolina* and *Artemisia*. I scattered seed of the Peruvian Lily (*Alstroemeria ligtu* hybrids) which flourish in the warm, free-draining soil, and now seed themselves into their neighbours.

Other interesting verticals are formed with *Asphodelus albus*, followed by the yellow asphodelines. The Foxtail Lily (*Eremurus robustus*) stands out well against the clipped Leylandii hedge, and so too do great cloudy masses of honey-scented *Crambe cordifolia*.

Additional background trees and shrubs have been chosen to provide good form and contrast of foliage. They include a Chinese Wild Apple (*Malus hupehensis*), *Rosa glauca*, *Genista aetnensis* and *Crataegus prunifolia*, whose polished leaves turn the most vivid red in autumn.

The border did not start off as large as it is now. Borders never do. To begin with, a border will be small, then in a year or two, when I can see how much better it would look if it were wider and how many more plants I could show and use if it were enlarged, out come the hosepipes which I use to reshape the edges of my borders. I sometimes mow a gentle curve. If I do not have time to move the turf at once, I take a half-moon blade (used to cut the edges of the grass), cut two lines on either side of the hosepipe and then peel off the narrow strip of turf that is left, leaving a clear,

Artemisia x latiloba 'Valerie Finnis'

Eryngium x zabelii

Crambe maritimum

newly marked edge which can lie there until someone has time to dig the additional piece of bed. I usually make any new edges in late autumn while it is still warm enough to stand around and decide the new shapes for the borders. Then we have all winter, when conditions are suitable, to dig up to the new line.

As far as the overall planting of the border itself is concerned, it is still very simple to maintain. As a low-maintenance border, it could be copied by anyone who has to garden on a fairly large scale – perhaps for a farm entrance or a long drive. There are not so many neglected farm entrances today but when I was a child I saw plenty, with rusty machinery lying abandoned among nettles.

Most of the autumn tidying up is for aesthetic reasons, but in some cases it is better to leave the tops of the plants for protection in winter. It can be quite difficult to decide what should be left so that the garden retains some interest. But if you have planted the garden with forethought, it should still look good even when most of the summer performers have died down or been removed. When I walk round the water gardens in winter, I have to rely entirely on my memory of what was there, but almost all the bones of the planting of the entrance border remain and the only things to

Among the most admired plants in midsummer are the Alstroemeria ligtu *hybrids. Each 90cm/3ft stem carries up to twenty-four small lily-like flowers in shades of pink, rose, apricot or buff, each intensified by two projecting tongues of flame, stiff orange segments striped with dark red. Here they are surrounded by the yellow-green bracts and ripening seed-heads of* Euphorbia coral-loides, *while the white-flowered form of* Lychnis coronaria *has seeded among them. Alstroemerias like a warm position in well-drained light soil. Their thick roots, like white candles, resent disturbance, so they are best planted either as pot-grown plants or from seed scattered into the border when ripe.*

have disappeared will be the collapsing stems of the summer-flowering plants.

One of the summer-long features in this border is the big artichoke-like plant, the Cardoon (*Cynara cardunculus*), with its graceful arching sprays of silver-grey foliage. When these become battered and damaged they have to be removed, as do the fennel heads before they have seeded. *Sedum* 'Autumn Joy' still has good form and deep colour even in January, and sometimes I leave it standing all winter. *Bergenia* leaves also look attractive all winter, with luck. Some of them turn red and yellow in late autumn before they die, but others remain throughout the winter, and will flush to rich shades of cherry-red and plum at the first winter chill.

Now it is established, this border does not take a great deal of time and effort to maintain. It is weeded only three or four times during the year. It helps tremendously in the beginning to cover the soil between the plants with a mulch, to conserve the moisture and repress the germination of weed seedlings. I use straw towards the back of my shrub borders, and pulverized bark among the smaller herbaceous plants. I do not mind a certain amount of untidiness – skeleton remains of plants can often be rather charming, especially when rimed with hoar frost – but once the garden becomes battered with equinoctial gales and rain, it is a relief to clear away fallen and rotting remains.

When I first made this bed, I did not necessarily use the ideal backbone structure of trees and shrubs because at the time I could not afford to buy a great quantity. I tended, as I have done so often, to grow what I could from seeds or from cuttings. But over the years the plants have grown, and changes have been made. Some were too close together, others were damaged by storms and had to be removed. Once you have finished mourning the loss of favourite plants, it can be exciting to realize that you now have the space for something new. Some years I walk round with a plant or shrub or tree in my hand, wondering where I can put it. Often we make mistakes. Take the form of Mountain Ash (*Sorbus hupehensis*) that I planted here, for example. Although it does not generally like such dry conditions as we have here, the last few summers have been wet, so it has done comparatively well.

The Golden Privet (*Ligustrum ovalifolium* 'Aureum') – a very common and ill-treated plant – growing on the east-facing opposite border I count among the successes, when it is grown into a

The large thistle-like flower belongs to the Cardoon, Cynara cardunculus, *and is related to the French artichoke. I use it for the architectural effect of its huge, jagged, silvery-green leaves which form a majestic arching clump several feet across. Stout soaring stems, set with leaves of diminishing size, carry large scaly buds which explode into a mass of finely cut purple-blue flowers. There is a much smaller species (which comes from Morocco) with more delicately shaped buds and flowers but exactly this colour, although it is not reliably hardy. It is called* Cynara histrix.

Part of the entrance border where plants have been chosen to survive low rainfall on free-draining gravel soil. The straight line of the 3.5m/10ft tall Leylandii hedge (× Cupressocyparis leylandii) *is broken here and there with other upright conifers and small deciduous trees such as the Mount Etna Broom* (Genista aetnensis), *the white-flowered* Malus hupehensis *and* Crataegus prunifolia. *The large round leaves of* Bergenia cordifolia *in the foreground do much to calm the fussy effect of small-leaved flowering plants beyond. Miss Willmott's Ghost* (Eryngium giganteum) *has seeded among several forms of* Achillea millefolium.

Miss Willmott's Ghost (Eryngium giganteum) *seeds itself liberally along the front entrance border. Not all seedlings can be allowed to stay, but here they are effective with the white-flowered* Lilium regale *half-hidden among them. Some years the lilies are taller, standing well above the metallic-blue thistly heads. To the right are two species of* Verbascum: V. pulverulentum *makes the tallest plant with branching stems;* V. chaixii *is more suited to small borders. Beyond the* Eryngium *is a large patch of a broad-leaved* Artemisia, A. × latiloba 'Valerie Finnis'. *It continues to make bright silvery-white foliage for the rest of the summer.*

free-standing shrub, as it is here. In my childhood I only knew it in gardens as a hedging plant, neatly trimmed and clipped, and I never liked it. I always thought it a rather bilious yellow. Then, one day, I was passing a bleak yellow-brick Victorian hospital, which time had turned a dirty shade of grey, and on its north side I saw two or three huge bushes of Golden Privet. Nobody had bothered to prune them but they looked so much more interesting unclipped and so vivid and graceful in the dingy surroundings. This shrub keeps its leaves unless the winters are extremely cold.

On the east-facing side of the drive, the border looks narrower although, in fact, it is not – it is part of a steeply sloping bank which runs down towards the first of the water-garden ponds. It has more shade from trees than the west-facing border and the soil is more retentive. Again it has become primarily a tree, shrub and ground-cover border but with less herbaceous interest than the west-facing border, largely as a result of expediency. I cannot maintain high-level interest borders all over the place so I have to learn where to concentrate my energies, but it does have spring bulbs and shrubs chosen for both flower and foliage effect.

At the end of the border nearer the house is an enormous pollarded oak which is probably over 200 years old. It is a magnificent tree with several secondary trunks springing from the top of the pollarded main trunk. Underneath its canopy I have planted a number of good tough ground-cover plants. In summer the oak leaves make a complete umbrella so the soil can become very dry. For years I struggled to establish plants in it. Eventually I planted a golden-leaved holly, *Ilex* × *altaclarensis* 'Golden King', which has made a handsome bush. In spring now the floor is carpeted with aconites and snowdrops – *Galanthus caucasicus* is such a good bold snowdrop – with colchicums to come in autumn. Very good with the snowdrops are two arums, *Arum italicum* 'Pictum' (of gardens) and *A.* 'Marmoratum' (of gardens). In one place the two arums have crossed, giving me a new plant with much larger leaves but with the beautiful veining of *A. italicum* 'Pictum'. These leaves – at least 30cm/1ft long and almost as much across – start coming up in the autumn and are at their best in spring, when the green spathes of the flowers appear, and then there is nothing until the red berries of the autumn. These make a good foil for the evergreen carpet of Periwinkle (*Vinca minor* 'Bowles' Blue') which is edging the bed and whose little starry blue flowers appear in spring. Although there is not much flower colour here the greater part of the time, there is foliage interest all year.

On the other side of the bank, facing the water gardens, I have planted spring-flowering plants. The hellebores, in particular, are doing well. We tend to get excited about the dark plum shades, overlaid with a sloe-like bloom, but I have come to realize that although they are fascinating, the lighter shades are more effective in the garden – the pure white ones, shadowed with green, and those that have apple-blossom tones stand out much better, while the deep plum shades almost disappear against the dark soil.

The low-growing Phuopsis stylosa *slowly colonizes dry soil, creating a weed-free carpet on the front of an open sunny border. It makes a welcome change among many grey leaved plants as it has fresh green, finely divided leaves. The flower-heads are like small pink pincushions, composed of closely set starry flowers. From the centre of each emerge long quivering filaments looking like pins. There is also a form with purple flowers, P. s. 'Purpurea'.*

The Water Garden

Senecio smithii grows wild in the Falkland Islands and Patagonia, but we seldom see it in English gardens. It is a moisture-loving member of the groundsel family, but infinitely more distinguished. Standing 120cm/4ft tall, it can be found in a damp border or in the margin of a pond, under a few inches of water. The large dark-green leaves are heavily veined, while handsome heads, as much as 30cm/12in across, carry a cluster of yellow-eyed ivory-white daisy flowers.

Large areas of water can take large impressive plants (opposite). Gunnera chilensis is the largest leaf we can grow in the temperate world. It can be over 150cm/5ft across, supported on thick prickly stems so tall we can shelter from a shower beneath the leaves. There is another, G. manicata, which stands even taller. Next to the Gunnera is the Giant Water Dock (Rumex hydrolapathum) whose large clumps of tall narrow pointed leaves make bold accents by the pondside early in the year. The tall spires of creamy-green flowers do not open until late July. The iris in the foreground, Iris laevigata, flowered in June with large soft blue falls, like the drooping ears of a spaniel.

I DOUBT whether I would have made a water garden if I had not had a naturally wet site, and I have no experience of making such a garden in any other way – for example, by using pond liners and so on. Plants suitable for water gardens range from those adapted to growing in the water itself, such as water lilies and certain iris, through those found around the water's edge, marginal plants, like bog primulas, and finally to large perennials like astilbes, ligularias and polygonums which need soil that is not waterlogged but remains damp throughout the summer. For a water garden to look natural this transition of soil conditions must already exist – or be provided.

In the shallow depression between the south-west boundary and the house, we had a spring-fed ditch which formed the basis of the water garden we eventually made here. We started by widening part of the ditch into a single pond and initially we thought, 'Wonderful, now we can have sheets of primulas and sheaves of water iris'. But since we had not done nearly enough to improve the heavy clay soil, the sheets of primulas never materialized. Only a few big and hefty plants survived the original planting and it was several years before I realized I would have to start all over again.

One cold February morning the drag line, a machine with a great bucket on the end of a chain, arrived on its caterpillar tracks to make a new pond and suddenly I had to be crystal clear in my mind about what I wanted to have done, since these large machines can excavate so quickly that the geography of the garden can be transformed in a very short space of time. It is not possible to be totally exact about dredging ponds. I knew what I wanted, but the scene changes so quickly, and everywhere is reduced to oozing mud, that it has to be done with hope and faith in yourself and the operator. By making several ponds on gently dropping levels I planned to drown a lot of my problems where the land was

very waterlogged and full of all kinds of scrubby bushes and weeds, including willows, marsh thistles and rushes. We excavated fairly shallow pools, because the deeper you excavate the greater the piles of clay you have to remove. Some of the soil was used to make dams, thus forming four large pools. Because the clay was so dense down in the hollow there was no need to line the ponds or even to puddle the sides to make them watertight. We removed some clay from the top spit of land around them and added lighter soil from elsewhere plus copious dressings of any organic matter we could find to create planting areas around the water's margins. We have such a diversity of soils here that we can often utilize one type to improve another. The clay that came out of the bottom of the ponds was carted away to make the west boundary, where newly established trees and shrubs now grow very well.

You can make a boggy area in gravel or other non-retentive soil by sinking plastic sheeting some way down beneath the soil surface, just as your pond itself will also need to be lined with

Part of the waterside borders.

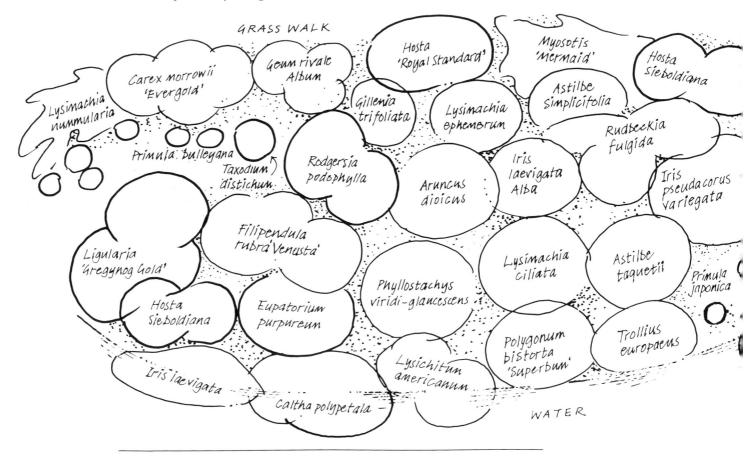

plastic sheeting. In order to grow the appropriate damp-loving plants around the edges you would have to put the polythene at least 60cm/2ft under the surface of the soil, but your choice of what you could grow would be limited. A *Gunnera*, for example, would not be supported in only that depth of soil. It needs deep damp rich soil, though its roots need not necessarily be in water. It can be grown on the edge of a very large lawn as a specimen or in a damp hollow in a garden. But it must not dry out. Either you have to water it or you need a reasonable rainfall in a really deep rich soil – an annual rainfall of about 75–100cm/30–40in. Never try to grow it in dry light soil.

Many gardeners feel the urge to make a small artificial pool with a few suitable plants around it. You can make very pretty small water gardens using half a wine cask let into the ground (allowing it to leak a little to moisten the soil around the outside). Use plants that look appropriate to water – rushy or iris-like plants, and something with big round leaves. Make one or two good contrasts

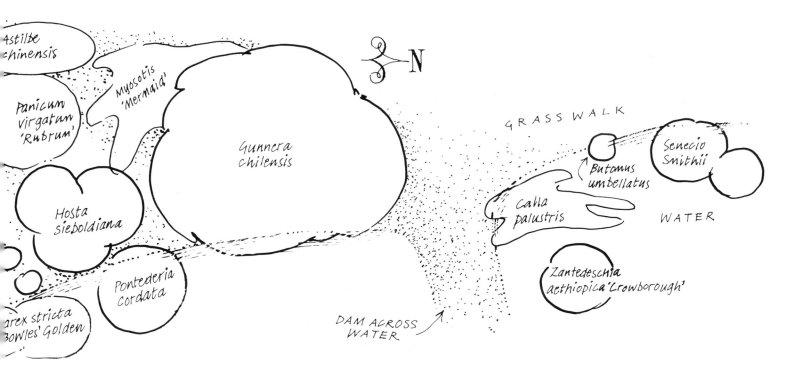

of shape, but leave it at that and avoid fussy planting. For goodness sake do not put in petunias! Garish colour is completely unsuitable. I saw an example of it the other day in a garden that I originally designed and planted. Unfortunately, without a firm hand to hold them back, the owners had slid back into their passion for strong colour. Where I had made a mixed planting of predominantly foliage plants (which was too subdued for their taste) these had been ripped out and the area filled with pink, red and orange bedding plants. It looked just like chicken pox against the green grass and flowing river beyond.

PLANTING THE WATER GARDENS

It is interesting to notice how many of the waterside plants have large handsome leaves. This does not mean that they necessarily always need a bog. It is sometimes enough to plant them in a sheltered area, in a protected hollow or in a dell in a woodland. These make ideal places for some of the large-leaved hostas, as do the north- or east-facing sides of the garden. In hot, dry exposed conditions such leaves will suffer, just as someone with a fine delicate skin will burn if they are exposed to too much sun. You can see that kind of distress in the garden. A period of ample rainfall will sometimes be followed by hot sunshine, when large leaves will

This un-named Astilbe *was given me, but named varieties in several shades of pink are available. They will not succeed in arid windswept districts. Moist soil and shelter from scorching sun prolong their season.*

Right: this group is not against the water's edge but in heavy damp soil that does not dry out. Vertical forms, like the pink pokers of Polygonum bistorta 'Superbum', *Iris 'Sky Wings' and* Iris pseudacorus *in the background, make good contrast with hostas,* Euphorbia palustris *and ferny mounds of* Aruncus dioicus. *In the foreground are the green-centred yellow button flowers of a double buttercup,* Ranunculus acris 'Flore Pleno'.

Large primrose-coloured bracts are sheltering clusters of small rhubarb-like flowers on the strange-looking spires in this picture. The plants are Rheum alexandrae, *belonging to the rhubarb family and found wild on the high plateaux of Tibet. In the foreground is a moisture-loving Forget-me-not,* Myosotis scorpioides 'Mermaid', *while the curious branched shape above the* Rheum *spire is the greyish-blue of a tree growing in the wide grass walkway on the far side of the pond. At its base I have planted the climbing* Hydrangea, H. petiolaris, *which has already climbed half-way up the trunk to display lace doily-like mats of creamy-coloured flowers.*

Left: the large rosette of leaves forming the focal point of this view is a hybrid between the American Bog Arum, Lysichitum americanum, *and the Asian form,* L. camtschatcense, *which has white flowers. The hybrid has white flowers in spring, much larger than either of its parents, but it is a mule and does not set seed. Beyond is a white-flowered form of* Iris laevigata *which makes chestnut-brown seed-heads to decorate the garden in autumn. In the foreground,* Primula japonica *is just going over but the foliage of astilbes indicates another wave of colour yet to come.*

wilt, even though they have all the moisture they need at their feet. Their stomata, or pores, are wide open because they have been accustomed to gentle soft moist days, so they have no protection against the sudden heat. That does not mean that they will die. Wilting is their way of protecting themselves. After the cool of evening they will stand erect again. *Polygonum bistorta* 'Superbum', with large dock-like leaves, behaves like this, and some of the ligularias will suddenly wilt in hot sunshine even though they may have their feet in water or in very damp soil. You may think how awful the garden must look because of all these big wilting leaves. But if they have been conditioned over the season to gradually drying conditions, and do not have regular rainfall, they will send their roots deeper, close up their stomata and adapt to the conditions as they arise over the season.

To sit on one of the grass-covered dams, surrounded by almost tropical-looking plants, watching little schools of fish sunning themselves among the waterweeds, and listening to the splash of water as it falls from one level to another is an unexpected luxury in

Above: the water gardens in autumn and early summer. None of the trees were here in the beginning except the Great Oak, seen on the left. I needed to plant more to frame the view. First I planted a Weeping Willow, Salix chrysocoma, given me as a house-warming present. Beside it stands the narrowly pyramidal Swamp Cypress (Taxodium distichum) while opposite, somewhat similar in outline, is the Dawn Redwood (Metasequoia glyptostroboides). The pond water is almost obscured by duckweed, to my chagrin. In the foreground, the bold clump of foliage belongs to the Arum Lily (Zantedeschia aethiopica 'Crowborough').

G. chilensis

GUNNERA

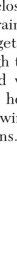

G. chilensis in late autumn, the leaves folded over to protect the crowns.

G. chilensis (scabra)
Found farther south in the southern hemisphere than G. manicata, as far as the colder regions of Patagonia and Chile, so it is hardier. Its leaves are rounded and more puckered and its stout stems not quite as tall. 2m/ 6ft. Zone 7.

G. magellanica
Usually astounds visitors seeing it for the first time since it is a low creeping plant with small round heavily-veined leaves hugging the soil to make weed-proof carpets in damp places. 10cm/4in. Zone 6.

G. manicata
Grows in deep valleys and gulleys in southern Brazil in rich alluvial earth and decayed leaves. It produces the largest leaves and gives a tropical air to temperate gardens. The fruiting bodies on its flowering stems are more widely spaced and are long and flexible like fingers. The whole fruiting head is brownish-green to start with but its minute round seed-capsules turn orange when ripe. 2.5m/8ft. Zone 8.

Two gigantic species of these plants are cultivated in gardens and produce the largest leaves that can be grown in the temperate zone provided they are given generous dressings of manure every spring and grown in very damp conditions. If they are not close to a pond, they need a large hole, 2 × 1.2m/6 × 4ft, with drainage material in the bottom, filled up with loam, manure and vegetable waste. They must be amply watered in summer. Although they thrust up enormously heavy club-shaped stems covered with pointed knobs, one never sees anything on these strange heads that could be called a flower. They need shelter from strong winds, and in winter protection for the coconut-sized resting crowns.

G. magellanica

the heart of dry Essex farmland. Lush though the water-garden planting is in summer, during the winter almost none of it is visible. It is not easy to find plants that remain evergreen by the waterside. Most disappear completely and there is a great contrast between the wonderful lush green of the summer planting and the bareness of the water garden in winter. In a typically English spring the *Gunnera* is one of the first plants to struggle to emerge from the winter gloom. The plants are covered during the winter months to protect them from the severe frosts. In April the shoots of the young leaves start to push through the blanket of old leaves mounded over them. Although they may be burnt a little by spring frosts, they usually start to recover by May and produce fresh green leaves from inside their great crowns.

The foliage of *Gunnera* and *Lysichitum* forms some of the grandest architectural features of the water garden. *Lysichitum americanum* is also one of the first flowers to appear in spring. Its foot-high spathes of bright butter-yellow emerge through the bare muddy soil at the water's edge, where they are reflected in the dark water. Soon they are joined by the flower-packed posies of marsh marigolds, both single and double forms, and followed by the candelabra primulas, their colours veiled among marsh ferns and little patches of silky, white-haired Cotton Grass. Crimson tapers of Knotweed (*Polygonum*) and feathery spires of *Astilbe* are the next to flower, while the rushy heaps of Day Lilies (*Hemerocallis*) have not only attractive young leaves in spring but rich-toned flowers in late summer.

The damp garden is spangled with wild celandines in early spring. I try to control them among small plants, but here in their native habitat by the waterside they do little harm and the sheets of shining yellow flowers are a delight early in the year while we wait for the main waterside plants to appear. Huge plants like rodgersias, hostas, globe-flowers (*Trollius*) and polygonums will later push their way through from a lower depth. Celandines are as pretty as aconites, and aconites themselves (if they will grow well for you, and they do not for everyone) can be invasive, so they too can sometimes be in the wrong place. All gardeners have to make up their own minds about what they consider to be a weed in their garden and whether they can tolerate it. What decides the issue is whether the plant in question harms the rest of the planting. A weed is simply a plant in the wrong place.

The lush growth of most waterside plants collapses and vanishes with the onset of winter. The wet margins remain bare of plant life. Earliest to reappear in cold March among scatterings of celandines are these bright yellow arums. Quickly following the strange cobra-like heads come the clumps of vast leaves.

The white-flowered Bog Arum (Lysichitum camtschatcense) found in NE Asia and into Alaska, grows in some of the coldest places that man can inhabit, where a jug of water hurled outside will be ice by the time it touches the ground.

Around the edges of my pools I have extended some of the beds to provide places for moisture-loving plants. At the pond edge the 'marginal' plants may actually have their feet in water, those like *Caltha*, the Marsh Marigold, among them. *Caltha radicans* is a later-flowering form, with smaller flowers. The double form of the common Marsh Marigold, *C. palustris* 'Plena', makes a good show, but I find the flowers of the single form more attractive. *C. polypetala* has much bigger flowers, but you do need a larger pond to grow it successfully. It does not have as many flowers as *C. palustris*, which is more commonly grown, but it blooms over a longer period. There is hardly a month of the year when it does not have a flower. The leaves are larger, too, making handsome mounds or rafts of round green leaves, eventually flopping into the water from the bank edges and continuing to root and shoot in shallow water. *Calla palustris* is another marginal, a little white arum-like plant that floats in the water. There are several kinds of iris – including the beautiful *Iris pseudacorus* 'Variegatus' with its yellow leaves – that will grow in shallow water.

At the edge of the pond are fine colonies of Pickerel Weed (*Pontederia cordata*), which slowly spreads into deeper water,

Marsh marigolds (left) are related to buttercups but need really moist, even boggy, soil. This picture shows Caltha polypetala, *a fine plant for large ponds. It does not create such a closely packed posy of flowers as other marsh marigolds do, but the individual flowers are larger and are flung out from among the foliage with gay abandon over months during the summer. The chief value of the plant lies in the great rafts of rich round leaves which spread out from the pond edge and root into shallow water, ideal for furnishing the bare edges of large ponds. A few clumps of* Iris pseudacorus, *whether the variegated form or* I. p. *'Bastardii', with green leaves and pale yellow flowers, planted among them will create a simple but perfect waterside scene.*

Caltha palustris *is the beautiful Marsh Marigold or King Cup, still occasionally seen wild in damp or boggy meadows. Well placed by the pond margin it makes a large display of shining yellow flowers in early spring. The white form, C. p. 'Alba', opens its first flowers before any of the others, still producing fresh white cups when its first flowers are setting ripe seed.*

forming crowded stems of spear-shaped leaves and spikes of small blue flowers in late summer. At the very edge in the squelchy sodden mud are the two magnificent bog arums, *Lysichitum americanum* (already mentioned) and the white-flowered species from Siberia and Japan, *L. camtschatcense*. The spathe is a big, handsome, modified bract enfolding the spadix, or seed-head, which swells to form a club-like structure.

Plants needing the most moisture must be planted either in the shallow water or within a short distance of the water's edge. Water does not travel very far sideways in the soil. The Water Forget-me-not (*Myosotis scorpioides*) makes a good edging plant against the water, its bright blue flowers blooming for weeks on end in summer. In places I have widened the border so that I can grow more damp-loving plants, while as you move farther away still from the water's edge the conditions are more like the borders in the Open Walks (which I talk about on page 78). That is, they are retentive of moisture, but not waterlogged.

Near the edges of the pools there are plants that must have constant moisture, like the big ligularias, whose large round leaves may be green or purple, several different kinds of polygonums, and many forms of water iris, as well as *Zantedeschia aethiopica*, the handsome white Arum Lily that you often see in church flower arrangements at Easter. This plant does well in 30–60cm/1–2ft of water where its roots are protected in deep mud from winter cold. Rodgersias enjoy the wet soil in open conditions but will also grow well in part-shade, in damp situations. They are among the most

Handsome by water or in deep rich retentive soil in an open spot, Ligularia steno-cephala 'The Rocket' *makes a sensational plant in late summer. Here it is backed by a light green bamboo (*Phyllostachys viridi-glaucescens*), while to the right can be seen the 2.1m/7ft tall stems of* Eupatorium purpureum *which will take over in autumn with wide flat heads of fluffy cinnamon-pink flowers. In the foreground can be seen the pink heads of* Filipendula palmata 'Elegans'.

*I have seen crowds of arum lilies (*Zantedeschia aethiopica, right) *growing wild along roadsides and in stream beds in South Africa, in the cooler winter season before the heat of summer dries up the watercourses so that the leafy plants collapse and remain dormant until the rains come again. In our climate it is the cold which causes dormancy – or death if the plants are frozen. Though they formerly had to be grown in heated greenhouses, there are now several forms that can be grown outside, if care is taken. This picture shows* Z. a. 'Crowborough'. *It can be grown in an open sunny border provided the soil is well prepared so it will not suffer from drought. Before the onset of winter the thick rhizomes must be well protected with a thick mulch.*

WATERSIDE GRASSES & RUSHES

I tend to use the following grasses and grass-like plants by my pondsides, but not all at the water's edge. Some are much better sited well above the boggy soil, but still in soil that does not dry out and where their imposing height and shape create fine architectural effect. I am thinking of the *Miscanthus* which could also be used in good average soil well away from the waterside.

Grasses can be found in many shades, some attractively variegated, and some turn striking colours in autumn, erupting on the scene with brilliant gold or red. The taller grasses, in particular, are valuable as vertical contrast among lower-growing plants with large round leaves.

Carex stricta 'Bowles Golden'

Acorus calamus
'Variegatus'
Grows in bog or shallow
water, with handsome
sword-like green and ivory-
white-striped leaves
1–1.2m/3–4ft. Zone 5.

Carex stricta 'Bowles'
Golden'
A lovely sight by the water's
edge or in a sunny place in
damp soil. This graceful
sedge has bright golden,
grass-like foliage with
pointed clusters of brown
flowers held stiffly upright
in June. 60cm/2ft. Zone 5.

Glyceria maxima
'Variegata'
A handsome plant for the
waterside or heavy retentive
soil. Broad strap-like leaves
striped with white and yellow are warmly shaded with
pink in spring and autumn.
60cm/2ft. Zone 5.

Miscanthus sinensis
'Gracillimus'
Forms a clump like a slender
bamboo. Very narrow
leaves curling gracefully as
they lengthen are topped by
plume-like inflorescences in
autumn. 120–150cm/4–5ft.
Zone 4.

M. sinensis 'Purpurascens'
Shorter than some other
forms of Miscanthus. By
late summer the upper surface of the leaves shows
warm brown, enhanced by
the shining central vein
which is pink. Narrow
pinkish-brown flower-heads
appear in October, when
the whole plant becomes
suffused with shades of red,
orange and buff. 120cm/4ft.
Zone 4.

Acorus calamus 'Variegatus'

Sasa veitchii

Miscanthus sinensis 'Gracillimus'

M. sinensis 'Silver Feather'
A columnar feature plant,
the tall stems are swathed
from top to bottom in narrow ribbon-like leaves and
carry upright slender
shuttlecocks of feathery
plumes in silver-pinky beige
to stand among autumn
flowers. 2m plus/6ft plus.
Zone 4.

M. sinensis 'Variegatus'
Quite distinct with its strap-
shaped leaves, strongly
variegated green and white,
which fall from rigid stems,
making a fountain all summer in a moist border.
1.2–1.5m/4–5ft. Zone 6.

M. sinensis 'Zebrinus'
Graceful stems in dense
clumps carry narrow green
leaves strongly banded at
intervals with yellow, very
striking as a contrasting
form in the border, marvellous by water. Easy any-
where in good soil.
1.2–1.5m/4–5ft. Zone 6.

Sasa veitchii
This ground-covering bam-
boo has wide blade-shaped
leaves, plain green all summer, but by autumn the leaf
margins become blanched
straw-yellow, giving a bold
variegated effect throughout winter. Makes dense
colonies of invading stems
so only suitable for large
gardens. Particularly useful
for binding clay banks of
reservoirs or lakes.
120cm/4ft. Zone 8.

Beneath the Weeping Willow a bed slopes up from the water's edge providing better drainage, though the soil on the higher level is still damp. The planting reflects this. Spreading into the water is the large Marsh Marigold (Caltha polypetala) *forming a group with vertical leaves of* Iris pseudacorus *and the rich green leaves of* Senecio smithii – *whose large heads of white daisy flowers are yet to come. Behind them in less boggy soil is the yellow Globe Flower,* Trollius europaeus, *and* Polygonum bistorta 'Superbum', *often seen in damp hollows in European mountain meadows. Against the bole of the tree is* Angelica archangelica, *while at its foot can be seen the lime-green heads of the Marsh Spurge* (Euphorbia palustris).

Candelabra primulas (top right) have a habit of intermarrying, so we have mixed colonies whose parents could be P. bulleyana, P. aurantiaca, *or* P. pulverulenta. *Their offspring come in mixed 'art' shades, including apricot, orange, pink and mauve. The large grey-green leaves of* Hosta sieboldiana *make good contrast.*

The view (right) of one of the waterside borders in June shows candelabra primulas, pale blue Iris sibirica 'Sky Wings' *and the double buttercup,* Ranunculus acris 'Flore Pleno'. *Pushing up fast among them is the next wave of colour, plants that will flower from July onwards. Behind the primulas you can see* Polygonum amplexicaule, *whose slim crimson tapers will flame for weeks into autumn. Broader and more savagely pink are the flower spikes of* Lythrum salicaria 'Robert' *while standing taller than either is a meadowsweet, a form of* Filipendula palmata *whose loose flat heads will be soft shell-pink In the distance, against the Swamp Cypress* (Taxodium distichum), *can be seen two columnar grasses.*

handsome of foliage plants. *Rodgersia aesculifolia* has broad bronze-tinted leaves rather like a horse chestnut, followed in midsummer by pyramidal spires of soft cream or pink flowers. Other species have variously cut leaves, some more finely divided than others, but one species, *R. tabularis*, has circular leaves the size and shape of a dinner plate (or even a tea-tray when grown in rich moist soil), while heavy drooping clusters of star-shaped creamy flowers held high on 1.2m/4ft stems are an additional bonus.

Under a willow beside one of the pools I have created an irregularly shaped bed that slopes several feet up from the water's edge to the mown grass walk on the opposite side. There, different degrees of shade and proximity to the water create very different planting conditions. In wet shade beneath the Weeping Willow close to the water's edge I have planted *Onoclea sensibilis*, a marsh-loving fern, spring-flowering primulas, hostas and the yellow Creeping Jenny (*Lysimachia nummularia* 'Aurea'). Higher up, perhaps 60cm/2ft above the water level, over the roots of the tree, I grow *Tiarella cordifolia*, *Galanthus*, other hostas and plants that do not need a lot of sun to produce flowers. Farther away from the

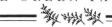
tree, though not where the soil is waterlogged, there are astilbes, polygonums, *Euphorbia palustris*, ligularias, *Angelica archangelica* and *Scrophularia aquatica* 'Variegata' – the big Water Figwort whose leaves, vividly variegated in cream and green, are among the first to appear in spring. This plant illuminates the border throughout summer as rigid branching stems continue to produce leaves of smaller size, but almost totally cream. On the upper side of the border by the mown grass edge, low clumps of a pretty variegated grass, *Molinia caerulea* 'Variegata', repeat this light colouring and remain a feature until the autumn when their knitting-needle-like flower-stems and soft arching leaves will have bleached almost to ivory. When the flower colour has gone from this border, a good display of interesting foliage remains.

It is important to assess the planting situation carefully. You cannot simply say this is the waterside, and so any damp-loving plant will grow here. Even in this relatively small bed of about 9 × 4.5m/30 × 15ft there are different conditions – in sun or in shade; boggy, or comparatively dry at the top of the slope.

As far as the ponds themselves are concerned, I would like to plant more water lilies, but the biggest single problem with my water is the amount of blanketweed which covers the surface as the weather becomes warmer. The conditions are aggravated by too much nitrogen, and I cannot get the ecological balance of the pond right. Unfortunately, the nitrogen comes from the farmland around. Although I keep ducks to try and keep the weed down, I would need to be a duck farmer to keep it under control, and then I would have no plants left in the garden. Algicides would control it, but then I fear I would lose some of my oxygenating plants as well. Lately we have experimented with two young men dragging a rope across the surface of the ponds. This removed much of the weed, greatly improving the appearance, but it will need to be done frequently throughout the summer.

Along some edges of the pond I now can grow the bog-loving primulas that first fired my imagination when I started the water garden. Among them are *Primula bulleyana*, with its whorls of rich orange flowers, and *P. japonica*, the first candelabra primula to flower, with heads of pink, magenta or white flowers with golden eyes standing above the huge rosettes of lettuce-like leaves. There are others, but last to flower in late summer is the Giant Himalayan Cowslip (*P. florindae*), whose buds and stems are powdered with

This shows the pleasure one can have using varying tones and textures of green. Enjoying cool shade and soil that does not dry out is the large-leaved Rodgersia podophylla. *Tangled among it are sprays of the tiny flowers of* Alchemilla mollis *which will grow in a wide range of conditions, but not in the driest of soils. There are other rodgersias, all with handsome leaves and tall heads of* Spiraea-*like flowers in cream or pink.* Rodgersia tabularis *has large round leaves with slightly scalloped edges, and a dimple in the centre where each leaf joins the stalk.*

Although the two pictures (above and right) appear similar there is a different atmosphere in each one, created by different colour combinations. In the upper picture the pale pink pokers of Polygonum bistorta 'Super-bum' *form a cool harmony with the yellow leaves of the arching shrub* Physocarpus opulifolius 'Luteus'. *In the background is one of my few rhododendrons,* Rhododendron 'Sappho'. *Slender leaves of* Iris chrysographes *repeat the vertical lines of the* Polygonum.
In the picture right, the colours seem warmer, despite the cool intervening fronds of the Ostrich Plume Fern (Matteuccia struthiopteris). Euphorbia griffithii 'Dixter' *forms an analogous harmony with the sunburst shape and yellow leaves of* Physocarpus. *Seen among the orange-red flowers is another damp-loving spurge,* Euphorbia palustris, *with typical lime-green heads.*

Left: this is the part of the damp border situated near a spring which comes to the surface and is lead into the farm reservoir just beyond. It is early in the year, about the middle of May. Trollius europaeus is in flower in the foreground with the maple-like leaves of Kirengeshoma palmata showing behind it. Not until September–October will the dark purple-stemmed flowering shaft droop with the weight of butter-yellow flowers, half-opening like slender shuttlecocks. The Ostrich Plume Fern (Matteuccia struthiopteris) loves this damp, partly shaded place, and is establishing a colony here. The yellow-leaved shrub is Sambucus racemosa 'Plumosa Aurea'. This is a form of the European Red-Berried Elder. Once established we prune it each spring, cutting out the long flowering shoots. If you leave them you will see the red fruits, but you will not get such attractive foliage.

palest green dust. Drooping heads of creamy-yellow bell-shaped flowers, which are sometimes well over 2m/6ft tall, eventually make elegant seed-heads.

THE CANAL BED

The Canal Bed is a large oval area of heavy wet land lying in the bottom end of the original boggy meadow, with the remains of the ditch (widened now – hence its name) running through the centre. The whole area is about 28m/90ft long by 14m/45ft wide. It is partially shaded by two oaks, the native oak (*Quercus robur*) that was here when we arrived and a Pin Oak (*Q. palustris*), which we planted. Some years the Pin Oak turns red, especially its growing shoots, in autumn and it is growing better than the native oak. Beneath these are mixed shrubs to give bulk to the planting, including *Acer palmatum* and the beautiful lace-cap viburnum, *V. plicatum* 'Mariesii'.

Initially I made narrow borders along the banks on either side of the ditch, but immediately I ran into two problems. The first was the quality of the soil, which was harsh and sticky – a combination of clay and stone with very little humus in it – and very unkind to the plants. I did my best by putting compost into the holes where I was putting plants such as water irises, primulas, marsh marigolds and so on. I also planted *Rheum palmatum* because I had read that ornamental rhubarbs like to be on the edge of the water, but they died; their starchy crowns rotted away, as it was too wet for them. The lower edge of the bank obviously was waterlogged. If you want

A sad little picture taken almost at the end of the garden carnival, when autumn leaves drift over the surface of the water, making ever-changing patterns. Although this scum of duckweed may add to the design, it, together with blanketweed, is a continuous worry through the summer since our water is too heavily impregnated with nitrogen that has been applied to crops on neighbouring farms. It is not possible to achieve an ecological balance so we are obliged at times to resort to using an algicide.

to have rheums near water, where their large leaves look so effective, put them some distance from the water itself so that they are not going to be flooded in winter or overly wet at any time, and provide good rich vegetable-type garden soil. *Gunnera*, on the other hand, is growing by the water's edge and comes to no harm from the wet conditions.

The second problem I found was that the soil on the sloping banks slid into the water. Native weeds, like rushes, certain forms of grass and the form of Willow Herb called Codlins and Cream quickly carpeted the soil, and I spent my time pulling out great barrow-loads to rescue the plants I hoped to establish. By doing so, I pulled off what little topsoil there was, and the sloping sides of the banks crumbled and fell into the water. We overcame this in an unusual way. We supported the pond edges by using hollow concrete blocks, standing two or three on top of each other to form a wall against the bank, and then drove angle-irons through them into the firm soil below the wet mud. The angle-irons were rescued from the farm (they can be bought second-hand) and we bought hollow concrete blocks from a builders' supplier. If they are available and not prohibitively expensive, wooden stakes driven to within a few inches of the surface of the water do the job just as effectively and look most attractive. We have now managed to prevent the topsoil sliding down into the water while the concrete edging, just above the water, has eventually weathered to an unobtrusive mossy green.

Opposite: this is a favourite view in the garden, standing on the grass-covered dam, looking down into the Canal Bed (below left) which lies on either side of the water. Although there is usually something in flower, much of the interest lies in contrasting forms, textures and colours of leaves. Beneath the grey shrubs in the foreground the Dwarf Periwinkle (Vinca minor 'Bowles' Blue') makes contrast and good ground cover, needing only to be clipped after flowering to encourage plenty of fresh flowering shoots. To the right is Salix repens 'Argentea', pruned after its yellow catkins have faded to ensure plenty of long and graceful wands for the following spring.
The slower-growing willow to the left is Salix lanata with larger, woollier leaves and large cream-coloured catkins. Beyond these shrubs the beds on either side are filled with a design based on good leaves. Moisture-loving ferns, the Royal Fern (Osmunda regalis) and Onoclea sensibilis, provide a welcome change of texture and form, as do several different grasses, creating a delicate effect. Adding small accents of colour in June can be seen Iris pseudacorus, Primula pulverulenta 'Bartley Strain', Thalictrum aquilegiifolium (both white and mauve), Viburnum plicatum 'Mariesii' with its layers of creamy lace-caps and in the distance Rhododendron 'Sappho' and R. ponticum.

I can now stand on the firm block edging to weed, plant or dig without the soil tumbling into the water. Ideally the blocks or wooden piles need be hardly visible above water level but sometimes this is not possible. You must use bold plants that will disguise the hard edge when it shows too conspicuously.

I now have *Salix argentea repens* forming a feature beside the grassed dam which was made to form the pool above the canal – this shrub looks charming all summer with long sprays of tiny grey leaves. In spring the bare branches are covered with little cotton-wool buds which burst into fluffy yellow catkins. Contrast is provided by large clumps of iris and tall Japanese grasses – various forms of *Miscanthus*. Even in early autumn after a wet summer there is still colour in the foliage and interesting texture. There are two moisture-loving ferns, the Ostrich Plume Fern (*Matteuccia struthiopteris*) and the Sensitive Fern (*Onoclea sensibilis*), which do well here because they enjoy the shade from the oaks.

There is also a form of the native iris, *Iris pseudacorus* 'Bastardii', which has pale creamy-yellow flowers. It has grown rather too

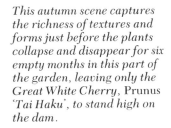

This autumn scene captures the richness of textures and forms just before the plants collapse and disappear for six empty months in this part of the garden, leaving only the Great White Cherry, Prunus *'Tai Haku', to stand high on the dam.*

A quiet moment in the Canal Bed, enlivened by the enduring yellow leaves of Physocarpus opulifolius *'Luteus' and one well-placed spray of the large-flowered King Cup,* Ranunculus polypetala. *There is scarcely a month in the year when we cannot find a bloom or two tucked somewhere among these great clumps of large circular leaves, provided the winter is not too severe.*

A storm has toppled some of the vertical stems of Lythrum salicaria *but their vivid rose-purple spires still make strong contrast against the bright yellow foliage of* Physocarpus opulifolius *'Luteus'. Balancing the scene on the left, the yellow is repeated in the fine arching Sedge,* Carex stricta *'Bowles' Golden'. In the foreground the haze of fine, thread-like stems and minute starry flowers belong to the Water Plantain (*Alismo aquatica) *while the pink,* Allium-*like heads are* Butomus umbellatus.

big for its position, so a certain amount of renovating is going to be needed here, but without removing everything. I would like perhaps to put in the white form of *Iris kaempferi*. I look forward to redoing this border. There will be certain features that I would not be able to move even if I wanted to, for example the *Lysichitum americanum*. These could only be removed by killing them with weedkiller, and what a sin that would be. The roots of an established plant go down deeper than the length of a spade handle (we have tried). If I stood against a clump of foliage in midsummer you would see that the leaves are as tall as I am – enormous, beautiful, spinach-shaped leaves, held in a great rosette.

Probably some of the other plants will stay. The big beds of *Rodgersia* are fine, but in the foreground is a bed of *Vinca minor* 'Bowles' Blue' which was put here for two reasons: I needed ground cover and I did not have help to cope with a more intricate planting scheme. Now I can remove it and improve the soil, giving me some empty space to furnish with new plants that have come in during the past year or so. The maintenance of this new area will be kept down largely with pulverized bark as a mulch.

I hope not to make a fussy planting but to find just the right place for growing a special group of plants which will enhance each other. I will certainly use more primulas, because originally primulas were planted next to the water's edge and have been driven out by more rampant plants.

Iris pseudacorus can be found in several forms. This picture shows it as it is found in the wild, although we have selected a good flowering form, I.p. 'Aurea', from seedlings. Some have smaller flowers with narrower petals. The paler leaves belong to the variegated form. They emerge in spring, boldly striped in primrose-yellow and pale green, maturing to a deeper green by midsummer. There is also a form called 'Bastardii' with attractive pale lemon flowers.

Rodgersia pinnata 'Bronze Elegance'

Peltiphyllum peltatum

Ligularia clivorum 'Desdemona'

Ligularia stenocephala 'The Rocket'

Butomus umbellatus

Menyanthes trifoliata

Pontederia cordata

In a way planting is like creating a painting. I will scrub out a piece here, saying perhaps that I could improve this by putting in a focal point here, or calm that by using something simpler. I am also acquiring new plants that need homes, but I find you cannot just take two or three plants and put them in among established ones. It is almost as if the old club will not accept new members. I think from time to time you need to renew your enthusiasm for a garden by making changes here and there.

If the framework is acceptable, then keep it. But empty a border sufficiently so that you can make a really good job of digging. Here, beside the pond, it will be heavy compacted soil. Over the years I have been accumulating more compost from the nursery and now can afford to buy more materials. I also have several men to help, so I can consider beginning to replant the boggy borders again. Throughout a period of about 18 months we barrowed all the nursery waste, mostly a mixture of grit and peat and sand, soil from elsewhere, rotted manure and lawn mowings, to make an improved soil on top of the clay. If you have thick solid clay, you must do what you can to improve it – there is no easy way out. To improve the texture is just as important as feeding it, in fact (as I have said) I think it is more so.

THE RESERVOIR

The remains of the ditch running through the Canal Bed finally tumbles into a large farm reservoir. Our neighbour bought this reservoir from us about twelve years ago along with some of our land to plant a new orchard. Although it has its attractions (a sheet of water holding about 2 million gallons), one has to remember it is part of a commercial enterprise. During long weeks of summer drought, pumping will reduce the level considerably, so any planting around it must be predominantly of trees and shrubs.

The orchard beyond the reservoir is not unattractive – there is something fascinating about its orderly rows of trees – but I was glad to be allowed to plant trees and shrubs around the large expanse of water as they now make a pleasant view from the garden, half screening the ranks of meticulously pruned trees, and they also help to create shelter from wind.

There are oaks, hollies, field maples and willows – mostly British native trees. They must be given a good start; it is useless to plant them straight into soil with the consistency of plasticine. Holes need to be dug with drainage sloping outwards so they will not fill up with water which will rot the roots. If you have nothing but clay and your garden is as flat as the kitchen table, the best method is to dig a shallow hole, spread the roots of the plant and then cover them with soil, forming a low mound of it on top of the clay. I try over the years to make a new soil layer on top of clay, using grit, bonfire waste, compost and spent soil from nursery pots. This is especially helpful for the smaller herbaceous plants, but trees and shrubs benefit from it also.

I did most of the planting about twelve years ago. One of my men helped me and was very silent and grumpy about it, or so I thought, until I remembered that he could not swim and was naturally nervous of falling off the bare clay banks into the deep water. Imagine us, if you can, at the end of a winter afternoon, planting the young rooted cuttings and saplings. We could scarcely see what we had done because everything was so small in such a big scene, and we were not working on comfortable grass but sliding about on slippery clay.

But the hard work was well worthwhile. It is a lovely sight now, with a slight mist over the water, reflecting the fringe of trees and shrubs. It is not exactly Sheffield Park, but at least it is improving gradually every year.

This view shows part of the farm reservoir lying at the end of the garden. The large Weeping Willow was badly damaged by the hurricane in October 1987 but such is the power of recovery that by late summer 1988 when this photograph was taken the tree was looking much better. Through a ground cover of celandines appear snowdrops and dwarf narcissi, followed by forms of Helleborus orientalis *(the Lenten Rose) and various shade-loving ferns.*

The Open Walks

The Kaffir Lily (Schizostylis coccinea) *needs sun and warmth but must also have sufficient moisture to make its blade-like leafy shoots, some stout enough to form slender spires of cherry-red flowers in autumn.*

Over the years borders have been widened and large expanses of grass reduced, but not so much that the overall feeling of space has been lost. This view shows part of the borders made on heavy retentive soil where, on this open sunny side, we can grow plants like asters, astrantias and day lilies which would wither in our well-drained gravel. As the line of the border gently curves away into the distance so, too, waves of colour come and go, each month finding a fresh combination. Here the primrose yellow Anthemis tinctoria *'Wargrave' is partnered with the modest green and white flowers of* Astrantia major*. In June when the* Anthemis *began its long display it was partnered with the coral-red bracts of* Euphorbia griffithii *'Dixter', backed by an upright conifer brazen with new growth. The combination was exciting but not gaudy.*

ON THE GENTLE slope between the south-west boundary and the water gardens the soil does not dry out, helped partly by the fact that it is very close-textured silt over clay and partly by its being fed by moisture that comes from springs deep down underneath.

When I first began to garden here I thought it was ideal growing soil – it remained damp far longer than the lighter soils, and felt wonderful in my hands. It turned out to be far from ideal, however. It is what is often called a structureless soil because it is very close-textured, has very few stones, and the drainage and the amount of air passing through is inadequate for many plants. The cure is to trench the beds – to dig them a couple of spits deep, spread gravel across the face of the trench, then cover it with soil from the next trench. As a result the soil will be better aerated and able to absorb rainwater down new channels created by the stones.

I first discovered that this type of soil needed improvement when ground-cover plants like *Tiarella* and *Tellima*, which normally like a leaf-mould soil, failed to thrive. I thought they would do wonderfully well on this soil, but they did not. Nor did any plants with fine hairy roots. In times of drought they were unable to penetrate the packed soil and simply sat on top of it like a cushion, their roots shrivelled in the top layer – you could lift them off like a piece of ragged carpet. At first I did not realize that silt is so very different from leaf-mould, but obviously it is. I've seen *Tiarella* growing wild in the woodlands in America, but two factors are different there. One is that since the leaf-mould is not so dense as silt, delicate little roots can penetrate it, and the second is that it rains there more frequently than it does here, and that makes a great difference to what grows well. Here in East Anglia three months can pass by in summer with scarcely a drop of rain.

Wherever you live you are going to be faced with some soil and

rainfall problems, although not necessarily the same as mine. I saw a programme on television once about a garden in the west of Scotland where it so obviously hardly ever stopped raining that I almost felt sodden myself watching it. Some of the plants were similar to the ones I grow here around the pool margins – there were sheets of bog primulas that had seeded in the paths, with blue *Meconopsis* and spires of white *Cimicifuga*. A whole host of attractive plants grew there just like weeds because they were ideally suited to those conditions, but the poor owner did not stand a chance of growing the grey-leaved plants that do so well in a dry garden. We gardeners are all perverse: we want to try to grow what we cannot. Much of my life in East Anglia I have wanted to grow moisture-loving plants like astilbes but in my previous garden I had difficulty even with delphiniums, which will fade and fail without adequate moisture. All the time you wish you could grow

Part of the border on retentive soil.

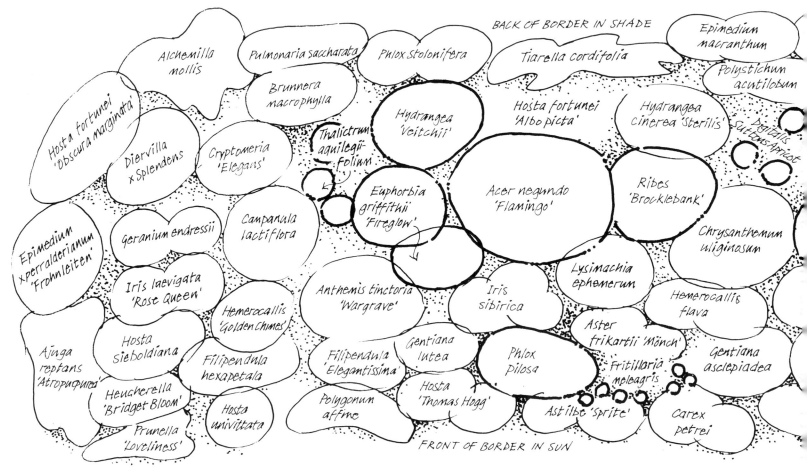

the plants you see doing well in other people's gardens, and when you first start gardening, this is often exactly what you try to do, without stopping to think about the conditions in your own garden. Perhaps you see something like Lady's Locket (*Dicentra spectabilis*) looking marvellous outside a cottage door in west country, and rush home to plant one in your dry, sunny gravel. Naturally enough it fails to perform. What you have not asked yourself is, are the conditions the same? We have 50cm/20in average rainfall in East Anglia as opposed to 150cm/60in in the west country, and this makes the world of difference. Even a small amount extra a year – at the right time – can affect which plants you can grow well and which you cannot.

THE OPEN SUNNY BORDERS

The area I call the Open Walks has three large beds, each with a wide sunny border facing the water garden and backed by trees and shrubs, leaving a narrow shady side facing the farm boundary. I divided the area into three sections because I thought it would have been boring to have had one very long border, and also you would not have been able to walk round each section and enjoy it in the same way. It will probably be altered again, as I want to create a winding path through one of the beds to create a mini-woodland area in its centre, where a tulip tree (*Liriodendron tulipifera*) casts some shade.

All three beds contain plants which enjoy retentive soil and the open sunny site. In spring there are bulbs, including our own native fritillary (*Fritillaria meleagris*), which is a damp meadow plant. Before we started a garden here that is exactly what this area was – a damp meadow – so they could have been growing wild here, although, in fact, there were none. But there were colonies of spotted orchid (*Dactylorrhiza fuchsii*) which we have preserved. There are also several species of *Narcissus* and snowdrops (*Galanthus*) as well as erythroniums, like *Erythronium dens-canis*, *E*. 'White Beauty', *E*. 'Pagoda' and *E*. *californica*. All these plants like deep rich soil that does not dry out, although they would not tolerate the boggy conditions lower down the slope nearer the water's edge. The bulb season is extended into June and July in these borders with camassias, from North America, either cream- or blue-flowered, which rise up elegantly alongside the soft tomato-red flower-bracts of *Euphorbia griffithii* 'Fireglow'.

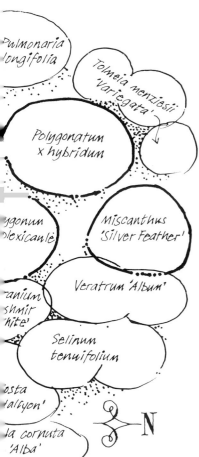

Pulmonaria
longifolia

Tolmeia menziesii
'Variegata'

Polygonatum
x hybridum

ygonum
lexicaule

Miscanthus
'Silver Feather'

anium
shmit
hite'

Veratrum 'Album'

Selinum
tenuifolium

osta
alcyon'

la cornuta
'Alba'

N

Smilacina racemosa

Euphorbia
longifolia

Geranium endressii

But the principal planting here is made up of herbaceous perennials and of course there are many plants which like these conditions to choose from. If you live in a part of the country with a good average rainfall then even in a poorer, less retentive soil than this you could grow the campanulas, astrantias and epimediums that flourish here, but as we have such a low rainfall in East Anglia then the heavier, retentive soil is imperative.

For ground cover in these borders I use *Tiarella*, which grows well both here and in the shade, as well as the various cranesbills. Most are quite tolerant of a wide range of soils, but there are a few such as *Geranium psilostemon*, a great big flamboyant plant with crimson flowers, which I would not put in the damp or shady parts of the garden. It goes far better with old-fashioned roses, or grey-leaved plants in the drier areas.

ACHIEVING HEIGHT IN PERENNIAL BORDERS

In spring, flowering bulbs and emerging plants create a low pattern of colour and cover, but by midsummer it is virtually a jungle as, apart from the edges, most of the planting in the bed will be from waist to head high.

Along with some other handsome architectural plants, I use the big yellow gentian from central Europe, *Gentiana lutea*. Its young

The last tree in the garden to break into leaf – Paulownia imperialis – opens on bare branches large trusses of pale blue flowers shaped like frilly-lipped foxgloves. The delicate white of Acer negundo *'Variegatum' is repeated in the layers of lace-cap flowers that line the horizontal branches of* Viburnum plicatum *'Mariesii'.*

This magnificent oak (below), more than 200 years old, has formed part of the ancient farm boundary for generations. It is the finest thing in my garden. Its strength and noble aspect support my spirit and put into proportion any pride I might have concerning my achievements. Beneath it grow cyclamens, species Narcissus *and groups of wood anemones.*

Betula jacquemontii, *a birch from the forests of Nepal, stands isolated in a mown grass walk with an open sunny border on cool retentive soil to the left, and one of the boggy pondside borders to the right. It eventually forms a very large tree with a correspondingly demanding root system, so is not advisable for small areas.*

HELLEBORUS

H. corsicus
One of my favourite plants. It is quite hardy but the flowers can be damaged by severe wind and frost. All through summer the stems form compact, shrub-like mounds of veined grey-green leaves. In winter they fall apart to make way for new shoots. In spring the large flower-heads of many pale green cups turn upwards to fill the gap. If well fed, they will grow in full sun or moderate shade. 60–75cm/2–2½ft. Zone 6.

These plants make good ground cover and are easily grown in almost any type of soil and situation, though they prefer retentive, well-drained soil in sun or part shade. They need plenty of water and feeding – shade the roots with mulch or manure to preserve moisture and feed with humus. They have handsome, large evergreen foliage and sculptural flowers. The Lenten Roses, *Helleborus orientalis*, look well in openings between shrubs or beneath trees where the scene in early spring will also include snowdrops, the marbled leaves of *Arum italicum* 'Pictum' and clumps of evergreen *Iris foetidissima*. The vivid lime-green of *Helleborus corsicus* and *H. foetidus* is outstanding in the garden for much of the year, so can be used either as foreground planting or to make an impact in the distance.

H. foetidus
This is quite different from H. corsicus although it has similar striking colouring. Clusters of maroon-edged, palest-green thimble-sized bells dangle above small neat clumps of holly-green leaves that are fan-shaped and finely divided. It has a strange winter smell. 45cm/1½ft. Zone 6.

H. guttatus
The name means 'spotted' or 'freckled' and there are forms with white or deep-pink flowers, heavily spot-

Forms of **H. orientalis**

ted inside with dark red. Some of the plum shades are peppered with very fine dark dust-like markings. 30–38cm/12–15in. Zone 6.

H. niger
The well-known Christmas Rose, cultivated since Roman times. Although reputed to prefer heavy soil it flourishes in my well-fed, well-drained, gravel-based soil on an open site. Rows of stock plants are crowded with blossoms in early March (never at Christmas). Several forms exist. We have one which flushes pink as the flowers mature. Others have green-shadowed buds which enhance the purity of the opened flowers. The leafy clumps stand about 30cm/1ft tall, the flower-stems rarely so tall. Because we cut off the old leaves in winter, long before the buds emerge (to avoid damage by Botrytis), they are not concealed. Zone 6.

H. orientalis hybrids
Also known as Lenten Roses. These produce the most sumptuous of late winter/early spring flowers. Their colours range from greenish-white, bronze-white and green-tinged pale pink to soft reddish-plum and deep smoky-purple. The flower shapes also vary; there are round prim cups, flowers that droop like ripe plums and some that open large petals to display pale cream stamens in startling contrast to dark purple 'petals'. They are easier to grow than the Christmas Rose. They like cool conditions in semi-shade. Flower-buds appear at the end of January if the weather is not too severe and the flowers last into April. 45cm/1½ft. Zone 6.

H. purpurascens
This has shorter stems than H. orientalis with smaller, neatly cupped flowers in muddy-purple or very dark purple, pale green inside. Included here is H. torquatus (of gardens) and among the best is 'Pluto', one of Eric Smith's hybrids. 30cm/1ft. Zone 6.

H. viridis
This is a subtle plant with deciduous leaves and saucer-shaped flowers of a pea-green shade. 30cm/1ft. Zone 6.

H. corsicus

H. orientalis 'Albus'

H. purpurascens guttatus

foliage looks a little like *Veratrum viride*, which in turn is often mistaken for a hosta when its basal clusters of leaves first emerge in the spring. Veratrums make narrow columnar plants set with stiffly pleated leaves and topped with branching spires of green, plum-coloured or white flowers in late summer. Fortunately, green flowers are more appreciated now than they were when Reginald Farrer wrote such seductive descriptions of alpines in *The English Rock Garden*. He gave a mouth-watering description of the leaves of *Veratrum* which built you up to anticipate a marvellous plant, and then dismissed the flowers as being of 'unmitigated dinginess', because he, of course, was looking for the bright colours so typical of alpines.

Nowadays, though, we appreciate bold forms for their contrast with smaller plants. Those which make this kind of impact include Solomon's Seal and the giant ornamental rhubarb (*Rheum palmatum*) which makes such splendid full-stop plants in this border. Rheums are sometimes described as being ideal by the waterside, but, as I explained before, they have to be planted on a free-draining slope. *Rheum palmatum* needs rich, deep soil – what I call good vegetable garden soil – to grow well. All these plants must be able to get through the droughts we have in high summer, when they would die if they did not have a good retentive soil.

Jacob's Ladder (*Polemonium caeruleum*), a very pretty plant with sheaves of small, saucer-shaped blue flowers and arching mid-green feathery foliage, looks well towards the front of the border. There are several species of *Polemonium*, providing flowers over a long season. *P. carneum* tends to flop about a bit, but although that might put some people off, I think that plants which droop gracefully, without doing harm to their neighbours, add such a pretty, natural look to the border. *P. carneum* is exquisite and flowers throughout June with silky textured saucer-shaped flowers, the buds opening creamy-white, then changing to pink and finally fading to lavender.

I do not like to see all the plants standing stiffly to attention, like soldiers on parade. I particularly dislike seeing plants tied up to canes and prefer not to stake my plants, keeping them closely packed instead so that the stiffer ones support the more delicate ones. There are a few plants which can be a trial, like the thalictrums. *Thalictrum delavayi*, in particular, does sometimes need staking because it is very tall and easily blown over. I try to

Astilbe
simplicifolia

Ajuga reptans
'Purpurea'

Geum x borisii

Unlike most of the euphorbias from the Mediterranean regions which will stand dry conditions, Euphorbia griffithii *'Fireglow' comes from the Himalayas and prefers richer growing situations, in retentive soil. Flowering May to June the jewel-like colour of the flowers is repeated in low clumps of* Geum × borisii *while a haze of newly opened leaves in the background of trees and shrubs, in shades of pinky-buff and palest green, creates a delicate colour harmony.*

plant it in among low shrubs and other stouter plants that will help to hold it upright.

I must admit I rarely enjoy looking at staked plants. If you visit some botanical gardens at the end of April, you see the piles of pea-stakes ready to go into the borders. The border planting begins to look acceptable only when the brushwood is lost among the new season's growth.

There are surprisingly large differences of height within certain families of plant (which are, after all, very similar to our own families, with brothers and sisters and cousins, close relatives and far-flung ones. The distant relatives may well have the same great-grandmother, but the similarities are far less marked.) It is much the same with plants. Take polygonums, for example. Some of them, like *Polygonum affine* and *P. vaccinifolium*, make spreading carpets on the ground, and then, at the other end of the scale, there is *P. amplexicaule*, which makes a bushy plant a good 120cm/4ft high and across.

I find people occasionally fail to appreciate the wide differences there are in one family, and when buying plants may well not look them up. Then, to their horror, the plant that they bought for edging a border turns out to be a striking architectural feature

instead. It is important to check what you are buying, and to make sure that if the plant you originally wanted is not available, you pick one which has similar features. Simply because it bears the name *Polygonum* or *Campanula* is not enough. There are several kinds of *Campanula*, including dwarf edging ones and tall ones like the statuesque *C. lactiflora*, which stands about 1.5–2m/5–6ft high with huge heads of typical powder-blue bell-shaped flowers. Some low-growing campanulas, like *C. carpatica turbinata* and *C. glomerata* 'Crown of Snow', with its spike of white bells in midsummer, are useful for ground cover.

Take also the gentian family. Most people think of gentians as low mats on the ground with beautiful dark blue bells, but *Gentiana lutea* is a dramatic foliage plant, standing 90–120cm/3–4ft tall, carrying stiff spires of yellow blooms – the only similarity with its low-growing relatives is the bell shape of the flowers. I try in my catalogue, as do most nurseries, to describe the plants carefully, but people sometimes neglect to read the entries properly. Coloured photographs in books and magazines, while delightful, can also be misleading since they frequently fail to give any indication of the actual size of the plant, especially in close-up. You may look at a picture of a plant and think it has huge flowers, but when you buy it you find they are surprisingly small.

One of the dangers you have to guard against when buying plants in a nursery is impulse. You are so overcome by the beauty of a particular plant that you do not stop to think about its needs, where it will grow, whether you have the right situation for it or how long the flowers last. If it is very short-flowering, no matter how exquisite, you might be better off with something less spectacular with a longer flowering season.

Another way to create different levels in the planting is to grow climbers over trees, particularly where there are no walls to provide support. I have a *Clematis viticella* which I am training up a pale pink cherry, *Prunus* 'Shirofugen', with flowers that do not last long. The idea is that the clematis will flower throughout the summer months when the cherry has finished. I have learned to do this from Christopher Lloyd, who practises it so successfully at Great Dixter. Elsewhere I had the white-flowered, sweetly scented *Rosa* 'Wedding Day' tumbling from the top of an old pear tree but that enchanting combination was felled in the night of the hurricane.

Opposite: forming ground cover at the front of the border is Prunella webbiana, *found in shades of pale violet, rose-pink and white. Above it, standing 90–120cm (3–4ft) tall, are clumps of Willow-leaved Gentian, whose arching stems are roped with deep blue bells in August. Behind them are the ribbed leaves of* Veratrum album *while behind these in turn the Martagon Lily (Lilium marta-gon) is in full flower. All these plants, including* Astrantia major, *grow wild on the cooler sides of mountains in the Alps. In the top left-hand corner you can see* A. major 'Sunningdale Variegated' *while almost buried are great bluish leaves of* Hosta sieboldiana. *Reorganization of this border will bring this bold feature nearer the front to form a focal point when flowers have faded and the border relies on foliage design.*

Campanula lactiflora *is a glorious sight when its clumps of leafy stems, over 1.5m/5ft tall, carry large heads of open, bell-shaped flowers in midsummer. If the faded heads are removed a second flowering will appear in early autumn.* C. lactiflora 'Pouffe' *is a dwarf form of this grand plant, its flowers about 30cm/12in high.*

SPACING THE PLANTS

Where possible I try to plant in groups rather than to dot plants about singly. But you can go overboard on the uniform grouping of plants. Carefully calculated groups can look too stiff and formal. Once the planting is established I like to see plants run into one another a little or seed themselves. I do not always plant in defined groups of three or five, but may drop one or two of the plants farther away as though they had seeded themselves. Even if I do not do that, nature will often take a hand and do it for me, and it seems sensible to let it happen, because it looks much more natural and more attractive.

Even in large borders, it is important to make the best use of the space, and you can do this by putting plants closer together than the books often advise, provided they grow and flower at different times. Many people make the mistake of planting everything the same distance apart, but successful spacing has less to do with how much room the plant needs than with what you are planting next to it. In certain cases, if you have plants that are growing at the same pace and flowering at the same time, you should not squash them close together, but you can certainly put the spring bulbs very close to the summer-flowering perennials. Different plants often use different strata of the soil. I have planted dog's tooth violets (*Erythronium dens-canis*) very close to the hostas, but they have finished, both flowers and leaves, by the time the hostas have made their leafy clumps, and their roots are much shallower.

When you are planting, do not think about the space as just an area across the surface of the soil. You also have an area in depth beneath the surface, rather like a sugar cube. Different plants use different layers and some will send their roots deep down, whilst others will sit lightly on the surface. Understanding of this comes from observation and experience, but sometimes it comes accidentally, too, when unconsidered plants seed close together and surprise you by their compatibility.

Thoughtful use of space allows plants to decorate the same area over a long period. In a small area, I have *Ajuga reptans* 'Atropurpurea' with our native *Fritillaria meleagris*, with chequered bells of smoky plum, growing through it, but mixed among them are the Kaffir Lilies (*Schizostylis coccinea*) which have scarcely broken the surface of the soil in spring but will flower much later in the year, in October or November. You need not think that because you have

This is the seed-head of Gentiana lutea, *a very different plant from its better known blue relations. From basal clumps of broadly oval leaves appear stout flowering stems, up to 120cm/4ft tall, carrying clusters of short, yellow, tubular flowers spaced at intervals along the rigid stems. Whether in flower or as handsome seed-heads gradually bleaching to soft beige, this plant has great style and distinction. It does best in deep rich soil in a sunny situation.*

Hydrangea petiolaris *planted at the base of* Paulownia imperialis *makes an interesting feature for months throughout the summer with its long-lasting heads of cream-coloured lace-cap flowers. By autumn they turn a good lemon-yellow before they eventually drop.*

planted fritillaries you do not have room for the schizostylis – they can grow together and both will be carpeted with the glossy purple leaves of *Ajuga*. Take another example: clumps of the little purple early-spring-flowering Dog's Tooth Violet can be found meshed into clumps of autumn-flowering dwarf-growing Michaelmas daisies and in other places have pushed their way through low-growing astilbes.

THE PLANTS THEMSELVES

Although they normally prefer part-shade, there are several hostas which tolerate open conditions provided the soil does not dry out. There are some (such as *Hosta fortunei* 'Aurea' which has a very thin yellow leaf) that scorch if you put them in sun, but there are a few others, including *H.* 'Thomas Hogg', with broad creamy margins to its rich green leaves, and the large blue-grey-leaved *H*.

Situated a foot or so above the waterside these plants are not growing in saturated ground; they will thrive in any sunny border with deep soil and adequate rainfall. In the foreground a double buttercup, Ranunculus acris 'Flore Pleno', has been tumbled by rain but it associates well with the pink poker heads of Polygonum bistorta 'Superbum' and forms of Iris sibirica in shades of blue and white. Creamy-yellow edgings to the leaves of Hosta fortunei 'Obscura Marginata' (H. 'Gold Edge') repeat the soft colour of Iris pseud-acorus 'Bastardii' at the extreme left.

sieboldiana which make fine features along the front of an open border (Hostas are discussed in detail on pages 124–7).

There are several different species of *Astrantia*, including *A. major* and *A. maxima*, that grow well in this situation. The variegated form of the latter has ousandingly beautiful leaves in spring and early summer. The flowers, quivering clusters of stamens with broad-petalled bracts surrounding them, stand about 90cm/3ft high and are attractive in a quiet way. Their chief attribute is that they flower right through the summer, with the added bonus that they press very well for dried flower pictures as the stamens spread out prettily like the spokes of a wheel.

I like to use violas and violettas among the edging plants, but not cultivated pansies with flowers as large as the palm of your hand. I grow the small-flowered carpeting ones which, to my mind, look prettier and daintier. *Viola cornuta*, the little horned *Viola* with deep lavender-coloured flowers only 2.5cm/1in across, grows wild in the Pyrenees, and I have seen it on the same slope with *Thalictrum speciosissimum* and *Polygonum bistorta* 'Superbum', all of which enjoy damp conditions.

Colour from flowers is passing in this part of one of the open sunny borders on retentive soil. Tall Campanula lactiflora, *sweet-scented yellow* Hemerocallis *and rose-pink flowers of* Geranium endressii *will be over by late summer, but a colour scheme and pattern of leaves will remain. The pink-and-cream tinted leaves of* Acer negundo *'Flamingo' show up against the dark green of mature oak foliage while great clumps of* Hosta *make a focus of interest among other small-foliaged plants.* Hosta fortunei *'Obscura Marginata' was formerly called* H. *'Yellow Edge', a good name since it described the bright band of creamy-yellow bordering the rich green leaves.*

It is October and the leaves of the Great White Cherry, Prunus *'Tai Haku', are turning lemon and amber before falling to form patterns on the mown grass of the dam which you can just see beneath the branches. In the shade of the tree grow ferns, hostas and Solomon's Seal,* Polygonatum × hybridum, *with the golden-leaved form of Creeping Jenny (*Lysimachia nummularia *'Aurea') creeping out to the grass edge. In the foreground are the pink flower-heads of* Polygonum campanulatum, *which forms a leafy plant covered with recurring blooms from late summer until the frosts destroy them.*

COLOUR IN THE BORDER

People often ask me about planning colour schemes for a border. In practice I rarely think in terms of colour alone, being equally occupied with form. If I plant a colour that jars, I remove it. But, oddly enough, it rarely happens. I suspect this is because I select plants for the situation and in nature plants that grow in the same conditions tend to go well together. Take the scarlets – the very hard reds – which are a difficult colour to incorporate into a planting scheme. They could be planted in the Mediterranean Garden, where they will be softened by the grey-leaved plants – picture the scarlet flowers of *Anemone fulgens* with the grey foliage of *Euphorbia wulfenii* in the background. Those plants would grow together in the wild and their colours offset one another – around the Mediterranean bright plants grow naturally in the grey stony landscape.

There are a few red-flowered plants which do require damp soil. In one of the sunny beds with moisture-holding soil I have a large group of a *Euphorbia* from the Himalayas, *E. griffithii* 'Fireglow'. Unlike the luminous green heads of other euphorbias, the flower-bracts of this plant are very like the colour of tomato skins, a beautiful orange-red. (This colour is enhanced by dark coral stems and leaves in the form called *E.g.* 'Dixter'.) *E.g.* 'Fireglow' is at its best from June onwards, and flowers for weeks on end. If it spreads farther than you intend it to, you can just put your spade through the wandering shoots and remove what you do not want. But in a poor gravelly soil this particular euphorbia would fail miserably.

A combination that pleases me in late spring is when the low-growing *Geum* × *borisii*, with flowers of the same intense orange-red, repeats the colour of *Euphorbia griffithii* seen farther away along the border, while both are enhanced by the many shades of yellow or bronze of unfolding buds on trees and shrubs, creating a warm haze in the background. At that time of year there is no sight of pink or mauve in this part of the garden to spoil the analogous colour scheme.

There are white flowers in this part of the border, such as some of the Michaelmas daisies near by. In the wild Michaelmas daisies usually grow in damp conditions. I have seen them right across America, on both the East and West coasts, growing wild – weedy little plants with washed-out colours and small flowers. They seed themselves like groundsel. Once, in Massachusetts, I was walking

This fresh-looking pretty plant with cream funnel-shaped flowers is a relative of two of my least-liked weeds, Rosebay Willow Herb and Codlins and Cream, both members of the Epilobium *family.* E. glabellum *is never a nuisance since it is not invasive and with me does not set seed. We grow it from cuttings. It quickly makes an effective front-of-border plant in retentive soil, but is not entirely hardy in severe winters.*

While the grouping here is not quite as I would wish, I think it gives some indication of the way flowering plants can be enhanced when ornamental grasses are planted with them. The Black-eyed Susan (Rudbeckia fulgida) is seen through the fine stems and feathery flower-heads of Molinia caerulea *'Variegata'. They appear to be placed in parallel lines and would be better if another plant of either was used to break the line, with perhaps a low carpeting plant like* Chrysogonum virgineum *used to make cover in the foreground.*

There are grasses to suit all kinds of situations, whether dry, damp or shady. Some, like the Japanese Miscanthus, *can be used to form tall elegant columns which catch the light with the slightest breath of air. Others, with airy heads of tiny, bead-like or fluffy flowers, add a new texture, softening the effect of many late-autumn daisy flowers.*

in a boggy area among tall reedy grasses and rushes and saw the big purple flowers of another form of *Aster*, growing with its feet almost in water. Many of the kinds we grow in Great Britain are hybrids – selected forms of all these many different cousins of daisies – but those that have over-large flowers and weak stems do not appeal to me.

I like to think of colour as much in terms of shadows as of true flower colour. It is the contrast between light and shadow in the foliage that is exciting – it gives the garden more atmosphere than if it had just been planned on flower colour alone, which is dis-

GRASSES & GRASSLIKE PLANTS

Carex buchananii
Although not reliably hardy, it survives most winters in warmer climates in average soil, particularly if protected with a mulch. It makes hundreds of shining stems like knitting needles in shades from buff to pinkish-copper. 60–75cm/2–2½ft. Zone 7.

Cyperus vegetus
Broad-bladed grassy plant with flower heads of curious green spikelets. Late summer to autumn. It will grow in almost any soil in sun or shade. 60cm/2ft. Zone 5.

Deschampsia caespitosa 'Goldschleier' ('Golden Veil')
This Tufted Hair Grass is one of the loveliest, either grouped in a bay among shrubs or rising alone above smaller plants. It forms dense tussocks of narrow arching green leaves and by midsummer many tall flower-stems tower above the foliage, carrying large airy plumes of tiny silver-green flowers. Gradually flowers and stems turn bright straw-yellow. Needs retentive soil in sun. 120cm/ 4ft. Zone 5.

Festuca glauca 'Silbersee' ('Silver Sea')
This little grass of softest powder-blue needs dividing and replanting most years in spring to look its best, but it is well worth the effort. Best in dry conditions in sun, when it becomes bluer. 5cm/2in. Zone 5.

I love to see a few tall grasses such as *Stipa gigantea* rising high above the mounds and cushions of other perennial plants around them. These columnar grasses need no staking. Their fluttering ribbon-like leaves or glittering seed-heads catch the sunlight or any passing movement of air. No other plant gives the same effect as grasses in the landscape, be they large and impressive, small and fluffy or graceful and fountain-like.

We often fail to make our garden designs as exciting as they could be and grasses are seldom considered as an important part of the overall plan. Carefully chosen, they add grace and elegance.

Stipa gigantea

Hakonechloa macra 'Albo-aurea'
A grass that never fails to cause comment. It makes soft clumps of foliage about 30cm/12in high, each ribbon-like leaf vividly variegated gold and buff with touches of bronze. Needs retentive soil and cool conditions, but not dense shade. Zone 7.

Helictotrichon sempervirens (Avena sempervirens)
Forms arching clumps of vivid grey-blue foliage and sends up oat-like plumes of the same colour. Useful contrast in form among other grey-foliaged plants. Requires dry sunny conditions for the best colour. 120cm/4ft. Zone 5.

Milium effusum 'Aureum'
Known as Bowles' Golden Grass. Non-running clumps of soft foliage, bright yellow in spring and early summer. Many fine stems support a cloud of tiny golden flowers and bead-like seeds. For part-shade in leaf-mould soil. 60cm/2ft. Zone 7.

Molinia caerulea 'Heidebraut'
Creates its own sunshine on grey autumnal days, with narrow columns of stiff straw-coloured flowering stems topped with dainty seed-heads. For sunny positions in retentive soil. 1.2–1.5m/4–5ft. Zone 5.

M. caerulea 'Variegata'
One of the best variegated grasses, with short neat tufts of vividly coloured green and cream leaves sending up feathery plumes. 45cm/1½ft. Zone 5.

Pennisetum villosum

**Panicum virgatum
'Rubrum'**
*A non-invasive, clump-
forming grass, tinted red in
autumn. Likes retentive soil
in sun. 120cm/4ft. Zone 5.*

Pennisetum villosum
*A beautiful grass with
drooping flower-heads,
each a tassel of fine white
hairs. Needs sun. 45cm/
1½ft. Zone 8.*

Molinia caerulea 'Variegata'

Stipa gigantea
*Tall stems carrying superb
heads of oat-like flowers
shimmer and shine as if
made of beaten gold. A
long-lasting feature for
months, throughout sum-
mer. Grows well in any
average soil in sun. 2m/6ft.
Zone 5.*

appointingly one-dimensional. The dark purples of the foliage of *Ajuga* and *Viola labradorica* make good deep shadows among the blue anemones in the spring and form a very charming combination with *Euphorbia robbiae* in a shadier part of the garden. *Ophiopogon planiscapus nigrescens*, a Japanese grass-like plant with almost black leaves, makes a marvellous contrast or 'shadow' with another Japanese grass which has leaves like yellow-striped ribbons, *Hakonechloa macra* 'Albo-aurea'; or I might have *Carex buchananii* shooting up behind it like a fountain. This is a bronze colour with no green in it at all which many people dislike but its stems look charming when they catch the light.

Usually I enjoy the gradual change in Hosta *leaves from green, blue or variegated to warm shades of honey and amber with, perhaps, a few overhanging leaves of Solomon's Seal that turn bright yellow before they all collapse in sorry heaps. But in October 1987 the garden was suddenly caught in a hurricane that appeared from the southwest, laden with sea water which spoilt all the foliage, burning it with salt. Leaves turned brown and withered on trees and shrubs before they had time to change to autumn tints.*

I think it is a good idea when planning a new border to make a list of the plants you will use, even if you do not make an actual plan. I like to have a list of the plants that I know will grow well together and look well together. This will include: the taller plants that are going to the back of the border (or the middle, if it is an island bed); the less dramatic plants which will be needed to set around them to show up the star performers, and some bulky things like hostas, bergenias or epimediums to act as buffer zones to calm a piece of planting or hold it securely together. I always start with my lists and then I go and look in what I call my 'pets' corner' where I keep the plants that I have brought back from my travels and from which I select ones suitable to the bed I am planning. I look through them all and may add others – from the nursery or from other parts of the garden – whose shape, form and foliage complement each other. I need a tall grass, perhaps, or a *Cimicifuga* or an *Aconitum* to make a vertical. I will need something bulky like the polygonums – *Polygonum amplexicaule* for example, which is wonderful in the latter part of the year – and then the shorter plants and the mound plants and so on. It is the shapes of the plants that I think of first, but I will also consider the pink flowers of some of the cranesbills and the shrimp-pink or flame-coloured tapers of various polygonums, and then I might decide it would be attractive to put in some purple-leaved ajugas to add a deeper tone – but not necessarily a contrast of colour.

If you concentrate on colour alone, unless you take things out and replace the flowers once they are over with something else – which is very labour intensive, costly and terribly artificial – the garden lacks other values. What I enjoy most in my garden is the contrast of leaf and form, and of course the promise always of the flowers to come. If you go along a border and see everything flowering at the same time, you get the sickening feeling, 'What is going to be here in three weeks' time?' If the dead flower-heads are all going to be cut down leaving bare stalks, that is no fun for anyone. Of course, in my garden things do have to be cut down, but there is usually something coming up to take their place. Or there is something so dramatic in the way of a foliage plant or another flowering plant that you fail to notice. I do not think you necessarily have to aim at having flower colour all the time. It is astonishing how a few well-placed and jewel-like colours among foliage that keeps its form and shape can illuminate the scene.

This October picture shows two giant herbaceous plants that must have rich retentive soil. The flat cinnamon-pink flower-heads belong to Eupatorium purpureum, *a sensational plant standing head-high. Above them are narrow spires of* Cimicifuga racemosa 'Atropurpurea', *whose elegant stems and cut leaves are stained deep purple. The small white flowers encased in purple calyces are sweetly scented. Other cimicifugas I grow will not tolerate strong sunlight, as this plant does, but need partial shade since their green leaves scorch easily.*

The Shade Gardens

Cyclamen hederifolium *grows wild in southern European mountain woods, so it will tolerate surprisingly dry situations in the UK. It flourishes in my garden around the base of our largest oak, where light summer showers scarcely penetrate the dry soil. In early autumn large flat corms produce hundreds of flowers in pink and white. Seedlings, assisted possibly by ants (and by me in spring, when I can easily remove the tiny single-leaved plants from the top of the mother corm), help to increase the colony. Many more of the sticky seeds are gone before I can find them, taken perhaps by grey squirrels.*

Opposite: sunlight glances down between the leaves of an oak overhead on to a mixed planting of shade-loving plants beneath the late-flowering cherry, Prunus *'Shirofugen'.* Trachystemon orientalis *is the large-leaved plant used to make excellent ground cover in shade and provide contrast with the soft ferny foliage of* Dicentra formosa. *Solomon's Seal (*Polygonatum × hybridum) *has made a large colony of arching stems around the trunk of the cherry tree.*

SOMETIMES PEOPLE who have a yew under which nothing grows come to me and ask, 'What can I plant in the shade of this tree?' The simple answer is, 'Don't try. Put down a mulch of some kind – peat, leaf-mould or pulverized bark, and leave it at that.' There is very little light under such a dense tree and – more importantly – little rainfall through it. Lack of both light and moisture prevent almost anything from growing in these conditions. If on the other hand you have a tree whose canopy is less dense – 'lighter' trees such as pines or silver birches, or even a mature oak, with glancing sunshine coming through its canopy most of the time – the shade will be dappled and some rain will get through, unless there is very little rainfall in your part of the country, in which case your soil will be dry. If you have a very low rainfall then the plants you can grow under a birch are very different from those that would grow there if you had twice the rainfall. You have to make a judgement about the amount of light and shade and the amount of moisture to determine what (if anything) you can grow successfully.

There are really two types of shade – the shade cast by trees and shrubs, and that cast by buildings. Near a building plants may not get direct sunlight, but they do get some light at all times. Plants in a north-facing border with a high wall behind it will have better light than those under a tree which makes an umbrella over them, so beneath that wall you could have more flowering plants (which need light to flower: the denser the shade, the fewer the flowers). Lilies thrive in partial shade, but they would not do well under a dense tree canopy because there is never enough direct light.

There are few plants – attractive plants – that will grow in what must be called dry shade. By that I do not mean bone-dry shade, but shade that becomes dry in midsummer, when the leaf canopy is fairly dense and only a little rainfall gets through – plus the roots

'Alba') and even some of the cranesbills such as *Geranium macror-rhizum* can battle it out together.

The first flowers often appear in January when the buds of *Narcissus minor* 'Cedric Morris' (brought home from Spain by the late Sir Cedric over thirty years ago) begin to open. In mild winters we can find plants like the white form of the wild primrose – *Primula vulgaris* 'Alba' – in flower in January, as well as *Helleborus corsicus*. Although this comes from the Mediterranean area, it is hardy in free-draining soil, producing shrub-like mounds of handsome, grey-green veined leaves and more green cup-shaped flowers than I have cared to count clustered at the top of stems about 60cm/2ft tall. *H. foetidus*, our native hellebore, opens its first flowers in this semi-shaded area any time from January onwards. Both remain handsome for four to five months, even when setting their seed.

Among the first flowers to appear under an oak or apple tree in part-shade could be cyclamens. They are lovely whether in flower or not, because their variegated leaves are so attractive. I have a form of *Cyclamen coum* with round, totally silver leaves, like a tenpenny piece. The difference between *C. coum* and *C. hederifolium* is that *C. coum* has almost round leaves while *C. hederifolium* has ivy-shaped ones. If you look closely in early spring you can find the newly emerging seedlings. If you part the leaves of an old plant you will find a nest of seedlings on top of the corm. I find it extraordinary that a cyclamen as big as a tea-plate will have a batch of new seedlings right in the centre. Isn't it curious that Nature sits those babies right on top of the mother plant where they can have no future? Some of them, we think, are distributed further afield by ants, who collect the seeds when they spill, damp and sticky, out of round seed-cases like leather draw-string bags.

Other plants that flower in early March are the erythroniums. The Dog's Tooth Violet (*Erythronium dens-canis*) is not in the least like a violet. Its mauve lily-like flowers look much more like cyclamens when their pointed petals reflex in the warmth of early sunshine. They are followed by *Erythronium* 'Pagoda' and *E.* 'White Beauty', two hybrids of American erythroniums which are taller than *E. dens-canis* and have yellow and cream flowers. I plant drifts of them under the trees and shrubs. Visitors sometimes mistake them for small lilies. Most erythroniums have beautiful shiny leaves, richly mottled like snakeskin.

Top left: when the drifts of snowdrops are fading, Pachyphragma macrophylla gives the effect of further snow patches beneath the still-bare trees. I love its crowded heads of tiny four-petalled flowers, especially combined with the opening flowers of the evergreen Euphorbia robbiae seen here. Just beneath the flowers is a handsome clump of foxglove leaves, but the most valued characteristic perhaps of Pachyphragma is its hand-some foliage. Large round leaves make conspicuous overlapping mounds. I have seen it covering yards be-neath trees and shrubs where no-one wishes to crawl in search of weeds.

Trillium sessile (left) forms the centrepiece of this plant-ing surrounded by a carpet of the ubiquitous celandine. This Trillium has three large oval leaves at the top of short stems, magnificently marbled in chocolate and grey-green. Dark reddish-purple flowers, whose outer and inner seg-ments are also in threes, stand upright in the centre, attached directly to the hand-some 'collar' of leaves. The few scattered white flowers belong to Corydalis bulbosa.

The last of my snowdrops are out at the end of March. I have an unusually large one that appeared about twenty-five years ago. It is scented, and has two flowers to a bulb. The Royal Horticultural Society think it is a form of *Galanthus byzantinus*.

Also out then is *Hepatica triloba* – a large rich blue flower that I found in an old garden. I am uncertain of its true name and should have it properly identified. I use a lot of *Pachyphragma macrophylla* for both cover and effect beneath the shade of shrubs. (It used to be called *Cardamine asarifolia*.) It is an underrated plant which slowly spreads, making bold ground cover with its large round shiny leaves, contrasting so well with *Euphorbia robbiae* behind it. When the snowdrops have gone, its crowded heads of white flowers stand out like lately fallen patches of snow.

Along the edge of wooden stepping 'stones' is an area that I have not yet finished planting. I must dig out the native celandines which are to be found everywhere in the heavier soil and plant some of the more unusual ones. We have one with bronze leaves called 'Brazen Hussy', others with pale cream or orange single flowers, and a pale lemon form with tightly double flowers.

This view taken in March is part of the little 'wood' garden shaded by a large oak and holly on one side, with a large Paulownia imperialis *and* Ginkgo biloba *on the other. The* Ginkgo *casts little shade; you can just see a bare branch of it cutting across the bole of the oak. Planted to cling to the trunk is* Hydrangea petiolaris, *which will climb to the top of a 15m/50ft oak if you have one. At the base of the dark oak are young shrubs of* Euonymus *'Emerald 'n' Gold', valued for their bright variegated leaves in winter. The snow-white flowers of* Pachyphragma macrophylla *look well with the lime-green flowers of* Euphorbia robbiae *above and apple-green clusters of* Helleborus corsicus *below.*

FERNS

Adiantum pedatum
A hardy, unusually shaped fern with handsome divided fans of bright green rounded leaflets are held on shining purplish-black wiry stems. 30–38cm/12–15in. Zone 3. R

Asplenium scolopendrium (Phyllitis scolopendrium)
The Hart's Tongue Fern forms open clusters of long ribbon-shaped leaves. Tolerant of most conditions, from very damp to dry, it will suffer in prolonged drought. There are many forms, which vary in height from about 30cm/12in to 60cm/2ft. Zone 5. R/D

Athyrium filix-femina
Slender and graceful, the Lady Fern comes in several different forms. They vary in height from tiny forms only a few inches tall to some with fronds up to 120cm/4ft high. They all need retentive soil and shelter from drying winds. Zone 4. R/D

A. goeringianum 'Pictum'
Delicate grey fronds, flushed with purple, held on purple-tinted stems. This fern needs a position sheltered from wind in moist leaf-mould. 15–23cm/ 6–9in. Zone 4. R

Blechnum chilense
A magnificent evergreen fern with huge arching leaves of dark matt green, it needs a cool, damp site in lime-free soil. It requires protection in winter in very cold climates. The roots are slowly but steadily invasive. 75–90cm/2½–3ft. Zone 3. R

Athyrium goeringianum 'Pictum'

Asplenium scolopendrium

Asplenium scolopendrium (in winter)

Dryopteris filix-mas
The Male or Buckler Fern will tolerate almost any situation except very water-logged soil and is the only fern that can stand quite dry shade. It unrolls elegant sheaves of typical light-green fern-like fronds that deepen in colour. Although not truly evergreen, it lasts well into winter. 90–120cm/ 3–4ft. Zone 5. D

Matteuccia struthiopteris
The Ostrich Plume Fern is perhaps the most beautiful for damp, even boggy, places sheltered from drying winds which brown the delicate fronds. Tightly rolled buds unfold from the top of short stems to form pale green shuttlecocks of exquisite lacy design. It is invasive, but easily controlled. Zone 5. R/B

Onoclea sensibilis
The Sensitive Fern has light green, broadly segmented leaves making handsome arching ground cover in damp or wet soil. It will also grow in the shade of trees or shrubs where it does not become too dry and where its wandering habit will be welcomed. 45cm/18in. Zone 5. B

Osmunda regalis
The elegant Royal Fern will tolerate sunshine provided its roots can reach water and does best on soil that is well fed with vegetable waste. The large flat fronds up to 120cm/4ft tall are soft coppery-brown in spring, changing again to warm tobacco shades in autumn. 120cm/4ft. Zone 4. B

Much of my garden is not suitable for growing ferns well as most need a cool, damp and sheltered site, but some tolerate drier soil than others. I have indicated the conditions required by the ferns listed below with 'B' for bog or waterside, 'R' for ferns needing ample rainfall and 'D' for ferns that can cope with drier soil (but still need shelter from drying winds). I am growing some of these ferns (listed here) because I have created specially sheltered and damp places. I find ferns invaluable for providing a contrast of leaf texture and form in the shady areas of the garden.

Matteuccia struthiopteris

Polypodium vulgare
This is a colonizing fern, making effective ground cover, and even growing on tree branches in moist climates. It is found growing on steep shady banks and in rocky regions of several continents. It comes in a wide range of varieties. 30cm/12in. Zone 4. R

P. vulgare 'Cornubiense'
This pretty bright green fern has much more finely divided leaves than

Polypodium vulgare 'Cornubiense'

P. vulgare. *It makes excellent ground cover all the year round and is useful for contrast with other simpler leaves. 30cm/12in. Zone 5. R*

Polystichum setiferum 'Acutilobum'
This easily grown fern has narrow daintily set fronds of great elegance. It grows almost anywhere that is not too dry, but responds particularly well to cool semi-shade. 60cm/2ft. Zone 4. B

The double-flowered form of the Common Snowdrop, Galanthus nivalis, *is one of the showiest for naturalizing. It does not set seed, so clumps must be divided after flowering while the leaves are still fresh. Here it is planted close against* Bergenia cordifolia *and the Hart's Tongue Fern* (Asplenium scolopendrium), *whose overwintered leaves are collapsing, to be followed by fresh bold leaves which will cover the spaces left by the snowdrops when they have retreated. There are several different species of snowdrops and many garden hybrids and variations. Some are distinct and to be prized. With others, gardeners need sharp eyes to spot the difference.*

The group of plants, opposite, on heavy retentive soil is in sun during the morning but in shade later in the day. On the front edge of the border *Epimedium × perralderianum 'Fröhnleiten' forms evergreen mounds of beautifully marbled leaves, in warm reddish tones, in spring and again in autumn. Behind are pale pink flowers of* Geranium macrorrhizum. *Other forms of this plant have rich rose or magenta flowers while clumps of scallop-edged, aromatic leaves make good ground cover. The curious candle-snuffer-like buds on tall bare stems belong to* Allium bulgaricum. *They arrived here as seed from the compost. I feel generally that they belong in the Mediterranean Garden, but they will grow in any soil in a sunny situation. The fern is* Dryopteris filix-mas. *The* Hosta *with large blue heavily veined leaves is* H. sieboldiana 'Elegans'.

I think you need to make a setting for small plants. Most of the plants in this little garden are species plants – that is, plants as they were found growing wild or perhaps first hybrids of them, which retain their original character. If you planted the large-flowered *Narcissus* 'King Alfred' in this bed, it would look terrible, being much too improved.

How heart-warming it is, early in the year, to find promise of what is to come. Lilies I planted as single bulbs last year are now coming up with three or four noses. If you give the plant every chance and prepare the soil well, it will repay you by flourishing and reproducing itself. People are often disappointed that their plants do not grow as well as they expect and it is usually as a result of not choosing the right situation, and of not preparing the soil adequately.

A good mat-forming plant is *Waldsteinia ternata*, with glossy, evergreen strawberry-shaped leaves. In spring each plant will be edged with sprays of bright yellow, saucer-shaped flowers. There are two kinds of leaf, large and small, on the same plant. Planted among *Waldsteinia* is *Arisaema candidissimum* which does not appear at all until mid-June but when it does it is worth the fright that it may not reappear. The flowers come first, emerging with their leaves folded around them like a cigar. An almost reptilian head of the arum-like flower then unfolds; the hooded spathe is

white with pink vertical stripes, and gradually the plant unfolds three-part leaves, each one rather like a huge clover leaf, sometimes more than a foot across. The plant does not grow very tall, but makes an overlapping mound, perhaps 30–45cm/12–18in tall, of dramatic outspread leaves. It is an essential impact plant beside the small rather fussy leaves of *Waldsteinia* and variegated London Pride nearby. From midsummer onwards the three together make an interesting design without flowers. In autumn the *Arisaema* leaves fade to the colour of honey before they disappear.

In winter there are still clumps of grasses remaining which we do not like to cut down too soon. *Uniola latifolia* is an American grass here making a graceful outline and beyond it is Bowles' Golden Grass (*Milium effusum* 'Aureum'), just beginning to make new shoots of bright yellow leaves. By early spring they will look like patches of sunlight falling between the bare branches. This is one of the few ornamental grasses I use which are invasive because of seeding, but since it seeds true, it is easy to recognize and remove, or plant elsewhere.

Creating a winter carpet is a little plant from American woodlands, *Tiarella cordifolia*, or Foam Flower – so called because of the multitudes of tiny fluffy white flower-spikes which appear in April. Threaded among it is *Omphalodes cappadocica*, a veronica-like flower with sprays of small, clear blue, and a really choice plant for cool positions. Ajugas do very well under trees and between other plants. Small bulbous plants come up through them and then die down, leaving the interest of a carpeting plant remaining. However, in winter itself, although many of the plants are not in flower, there is still a lot to enjoy. A lively patch of foliage is made by the variegated form of London Pride – *Saxifraga × urbium* 'Aurea Punctata'. It flowers in May with sprays of delicate pink flowers, but in winter the fresh rosettes of dark green leaves, speckled with gold, are to be enjoyed.

I prefer not to see large expanses of bare ground even in winter. I like as far as possible to cover the soil all year round, but there are some plants which disappear totally. If you have a proportion of plants which remain in winter it helps to keep the garden alive and if you can retain a few seed-heads or attractive grasses they also help to create little scenes. You can, if you search around, find plants to provide total ground cover throughout the year and places like public parks might well find it an advantage, but as I am

Corydalis cheilanthifolia

Pulmonaria longifolia

Pulmonaria saccharata

Polystichum setiferum 'Acutilobum'

Hakonechloa macra 'Albo-aurea'

Ophiopogon planiscapus nigrescens

Hosta 'Frances Williams'

a collector I like to mix deciduous and evergreen plants. I do not mind having a few bare spaces here and there – it is all part of the change into winter – but I find they look much more attractive if the soil is protected with a mulch. In certain cases, this is preferable to too much ground cover because plants can become overrun, or be damaged by sheltering slugs – you may find that the emerging stems of precious fritillaries or delphiniums have been eaten through. Such plants need an open space around them where slugs can easily be picked off by birds and other predators.

Epimediums are very good plants for shady places. There are many varieties, all with pretty shield-shaped leaves held on thin wiry stems, creating an overlapping effect which makes me think of German roof tiles I have seen that look like fish scales. Before the new leaves appear in early spring and the flower-stems begin to push through the old leaf-stems, we cut away the old leaves. The flowers are like tiny columbines, in either creamy-yellow or pink. Sometimes visitors say to me, 'Mine have never flowered'. They might think that because the flowers are practically hidden among the last year's leaves. If you cut these down you will see the little flower-buds appearing low down, followed later by a filmy cloud of tiny pastel-coloured flowers. When the new leaves unfold many of them are suffused with brick-red or coral-pink over very pale green. Then as the plant matures, the bright marbled effect fades

Snowdrops and dwarf daffodils provided flowers in late winter and spring on this north-facing clay bank, but now, in July, the design relies almost entirely on foliage. Large leaves of the ornamental rhubarb, Rheum palmatum 'Atrosanguineum', dominate the background. To the left long arching wands of the yellow-leaved Physocarpus opulifolius 'Luteus' lead the eye through foliage of Helleborus orientalis to bold clumps of summer-fresh Bergenia leaves. To their left is the silver-leaved Pulmonaria saccharata 'Argentea'. In the foreground is a superb blue-leaved Hosta, one of several unnamed forms we have which originated from hostas bred and cultivated by the late Eric Smith.

to green and forms part of the cool carpet of the shady garden. But in autumn the warm colours return and the green leaves become burnished with bronze and coral tints.

I also have many different dicentras in this part of the garden: one with ferny greyish leaves, others with bright green leaves, and some with flowers like Dutchman's breeches rather than the Lady's Locket of the plant's common name. Dicentras are nearly all in shades of rosy pink and white. Lady's Locket itself (*Dicentra spectabilis*) is quite a grand plant and does not run about like the smaller edging forms.

Another dramatic leaf in form and colour is *Arum italicum* 'Pictum' which grows here as well as under the pollarded oak (see page 45). In winter the leaves are quite small, just right to put with snowdrops or other early spring flowers you might pick, but by April or May the leaves are large enough to arrange in a pedestal for Easter church decorations. They are glossy, spear-shaped, wavy-edged leaves with strong silvery-cream veins. Flower arrangers love them and so do most gardeners. They like these cool shaded parts of the garden and will seed themselves true. Established clumps can be divided.

Where you have more space and are not afraid of something being a little invasive, *Euphorbia robbiae* makes a good all-the-year-round plant. It forms large handsome rosettes of dark-green leathery leaves and from the centre of each rosette there unfolds, in spring, a slowly expanding head of typical luminous-green spring flowers. The flower-heads can remain all summer and in some gardens they fade to soft coppery shades. *E. robbiae* spreads itself by underground runners and is one of the few euphorbias that tolerates shade. It is a good plant in a big garden, in a shrubbery, or under mature trees. If you have a small garden you might have to say a firm 'No' to it, but it is something I recommend to anyone looking for plants that show well in winter. It has good leaves for arrangements indoors and strong form in the garden.

Ferns flourish in cool shade. In East Anglia I am unable to grow some of the ferns from the Redwood forests along the west coast of Oregon, where *Polystichum munitum* grows as tall as I am and the rainfall is 150–250cm/60–100in. Gardens with wet climates are perfect for many ferns which must have a moist atmosphere as well as damp leaf-mould soil. Gardens exposed to drying winds are more limited in the number of ferns they can grow well but some ferns are tough and will grow almost anywhere. Perhaps the best is the Male Fern (*Dryopteris filix-mas*) but even that does not appreciate being put into a hot sunny border. It tolerates surprisingly dry shade and I have seen it growing well in the rooty bottom of a hedge. It is a handsome fern though not among the most choice. ('Choice' usually means more difficult.) I think the polystichums are more elegant. Several forms of the Soft Shield Fern (*Polystichum setiferum* 'Acutilobum') are both daintier and more elegant and not difficult to grow in cool soil when sheltered from wind as well as sun. A good form of our native fern is *Polypodium vulgare* 'Cornubiense', an evergreen fern, pretty to use in winter flower arrangements with *Skimmia* berries and snowdrops, if your rooms are not overheated. The species, *P.*

I think the picture on the left would make a good design for a needlepoint canvas. It is beautifully balanced, with the bright red fruits of Arum italicum 'Pictum' *and the spotted basal leaves of* Pulmonaria saccharata *making the central focus of interest. All around are varying shapes and textures of leaves. Behind are the sword-like leaves of evergreen* Iris foetidissima, *while in the background can be seen the yellow-spotted laurel,* Aucuba japonica 'Crotonifolia'. *In the lower left-hand corner you can see a pale green leaf of* Aquilegia *while the finely divided fern-like leaf is* Filipendula hexapetala. *An annual* Euphorbia, *a native weed,* E. peplus, *makes a haze of little pale green dots. To the right a hardy fuchsia dangles a solitary bud.*

The Hart's Tongue Fern (Asplenium scolopendrium) *is a British native, found also throughout the northern hemisphere. It will grow in any soil, including chalk, but needs cool retentive soil, being intolerant of droughts. Its shining strap-shaped leaves, arranged in shuttlecock formation, make excellent contrast with lacy-leaved plants like* Dicentra formosa *or rosettes of bold-shaped leaves such as those of spotted pulmonarias. In the wild, variations can be found. We have some with very narrow leaves, neatly gathered at the edges, while the rare form* Asplenium scolopendrium 'Crispum' *has broader pale green leaves with beautifully gophered edges. There are forms available with monstrous crooked tips. To my mind they lose all the grace and simplicity of the wild form.*

vulgare, has more simple leaves, not so intricately cut. The Hart's Tongue Fern (*Asplenium scolopendrium*) becomes rather tatty by the end of winter but I relish its strong contrast of form among either finely cut or rounded leaves.

Most people's eyes glaze over when I recommend ivies for poor shaded soil, such as an impossibly dry piece of ground beneath a dense tree. I myself have a practically bone-dry place beneath a great holly. Certainly the nearer you get to the trunk of a mature yew or a holly, the more difficult it is going to be to grow anything and mulching may be the best option. Under my holly I have found dwarf periwinkles and various forms of common ivy, *Hedera helix*, to be the only plants I can establish in such conditions. Ivies seem to grow in the driest places and there are so many different kinds with really attractive leaves, different in shape and form, as well as those with patterns of different variegations. I had a long bare bank of clay at one end of the long shady border which I have completely buried beneath shawls of different forms of ivy. It was such raw clay that even the native weeds could not establish themselves there. I dug sloping holes in the clay (so they would not fill with water), put a spadeful of compost into each hole and then firmed in the little plants. In a comparatively short time the bank became covered with green, eventually smothering the clay beneath. Now other

*An early spring picture shows blue primroses tucked among emerging blades of Bowles' Golden Grass (*Milium effusum 'Aureum'*). This graceful grass has leaves, stems and delicate sprays of tiny flowers followed by bead-like seeds all tinted warm yellow. In early spring the plants warm a bleak scene as much as if sunlight had dropped through the bare branches above. Another spring favourite, Arum italicum 'Pictum', has beautiful marbled leaves, a joy to pick throughout winter and spring to put with snowdrops, small narcissus, winter jasmine, or any other handful of blossoms to be found in the garden at that time of year.*

shade-loving plants are colonizing among the trails of ivy. *Euphorbia robbiae*, *Iris foetidissima* and *Euphorbia amygdaloides* 'Purpurea', the red-tinged form of our native euphorbia, are all adding interest and contrast of form.

There is not an enormous range of plants or bushes that will remain evergreen and tolerate hard winters. I am grateful for an ivy that I have which grows as a shrub. It is called *Hedera helix* 'Poetica' and it slowly forms a bush of only flowering shoots – there are no long running trails, nor will there ever be because it has been propagated originally from a mature fruiting branch. Every winter it is loaded with clusters of fruit. In the normal English ivy, *H. helix*, these turn black, but ours turn to soft orange in spring. In my winter garden beneath the large oak it makes a fine and interesting feature. I also have a Portugal Laurel (*Prunus lusitanica*) planted close to the bole of the great oak, and for a slim vertical there is an upright yew, but this bush ivy makes a small to medium-sized rounded shape which is very useful.

There are various forms of violas which retain carpets of leaves in winter, including blue- and white-flowered forms of *Viola cornuta* along the edge of the border. The leaves of ajugas may be slightly damaged by frost but they make a decorative feature. There is the pink-washed form called *Ajuga reptans* 'Burgundy Glow', while the variegated form makes a pattern of cream and green. A mossy saxifrage with finely cut leaves makes good contrast. Just peeping through the soil at about the same time is *Viola septentrionalis*, which produces large white unscented flowers. You can easily find the clumps before the leaves appear because the rhizome-like shoots lie practically on the surface.

Small evergreen shrubs well suited to small gardens are any of the forms of *Sarcococca* (Christmas Box). They like shade and make small neat bushes of glossy pointed leaves. From quite young plants you can pick in January, if the weather is not too severe, little sprigs of tiny sweet-scented white flowers.

At the end of the winter garden there is a large bush of the evergreen *Viburnum davidii*. It spreads out across the path like a great bulwark where the garden changes as the land rises up to an exposed gravel bank.

Here, if you stand among one specific group of plants, all plants that like cool, shady conditions, and look towards a higher level to the Mediterranean garden, where the plants enjoy sun in gravel

*This is the Dog's Tooth Violet (*Erythronium dens-canis*). It can be grown almost anywhere in full sun or part shade. The flowers need sun to cause them to flex back their petals. In this picture they are modestly hanging their heads, chilled by a sudden March shower. The beauty of their leaves lasts longer in a more sheltered situation, but both flowers and leaves are fleeting – all will have disappeared by May.*

soil, you can see from a distance the change in leaf types – the drought-loving grey plants like *Artemisia* are on the open slope, contrasting with the group planted in shade. If you walk up into the sunshine in summer, it feels several degrees warmer, away from the shade of the oak and the holly.

THE NORTH-FACING CLAY BANK

The bank of heavy clay soil between the Reservoir and the southern end of the Shady Walk grows epimediums well. For contrast I grow the spider-like Japanese plant with flat black strap-shaped leaves called *Ophiopogon planiscapus nigrescens* – a dreadful name. In winter, we can find clusters of shining dark purple berries among the black leaves: the birds do not appear to eat them. The berries are preceded in late summer by sprays of little pink flowers.

Hellebores are the spring theme along this cool border, as many forms of *Helleborus orientalis* are at their best from February to April and they come in many shades of plum, rose and smoky purple, while others are pure white or green- and bronze-shadowed. Most of them are from eastern Europe where they grow in thickets or on the edges of woodland round the Black Sea below the Caucasus mountains. If you are interested in hellebores you will discover named beauties like *H. atrorubens*, *H. abschassicus* and *H. purpurascens guttatus* ('*guttatus*' means spotted). When you tip up the flowers of *H. p. guttatus*, either white or pink, you see they are heavily speckled inside with maroon. Some forms are now being selected to hold up their heads to face you rather than drooping like lampshades, but I admire their modesty, and like having to bend to look at them.

Bergenias grow here, as they will almost anywhere. They are very adaptable plants and I find their large leathery leaves equally useful in the dry garden as full-stop plants where a hosta would not survive happily. Bergenias make more lasting features than hostas since they are evergreen.

THE LONG SHADY WALK

In the Long Shady Walk, where the shade is cast by a row of oaks, I have more room to grow bigger and perhaps coarser plants than I have in the small shade garden beneath the great oak and holly. It is the ideal place for many different kinds of *Pulmonaria*. *P.*

The double-flowered Lady's Smock or Cuckoo Flower (Cardamine pratensis 'Flore Pleno') picks up the pale lavender buds of Rhododendron 'Sappho', *whose open flowers reveal striking dark eyes.* Hosta tardiana 'Halcyon' *is one of the best blue hostas, especially since it remains a good colour throughout the growing season. The contrasting plant in the centre is Salad Burnet (Sanguisorba officinalis). In midsummer it will bear tall stems topped with small wine-red heads.*

This speckling of blossom needs a shaft of sunlight to reveal the true beauty of the large white wood anemones. There are several good forms of Anemone nemorosa. *They are easily grown in almost any soil in shady situations among trees or shrubs. They colonize quickly by means of underground rhizomes until spring, when the ground is suddenly carpeted with dainty leaves*

and wide-open flowers in shades of blue or white, lit with yellow centres. A. n. 'Allenii' has the richest blue flowers warmed by the plum-stained backs of the petals. A. n. 'Robinsoniana' is as lovely, but of cooler lavender-blue, since the outside of the petals is creamy-grey. There are also two forms with double white flowers. Several other dwarf anemones for cool shady spots include the tiny yellow-flowered A. ranunculoides and a primrose-yellow hybrid A. × seemanii.

This group, photographed in July, is part of the shaded border beneath mature oaks along the shady walk that forms our west boundary. The white and pink forms of Lilium martagon *grow together with the white-flowered* Astrantia major *'Alba' in front of them. The* Astrantia, or Masterwort, *has white and green daisy-like flowers whose wheel-spoke centres press to make a neat and fascinating shape for those who make dried flower pictures. In the foreground* Heuchera micrantha *'Palace Purple' remains in handsome leaf for months throughout summer and autumn, while* Hosta tardiana *'Halcyon' makes a river of blue beneath the arching foliage of Solomon's Seal,* Polygonatum × hybridum.

longifolia has long narrow spotted leaves. *P. saccharata* has the largest leaves, handsomely spotted. We have several named variants of *P. angustifolia*, all with plain green, bristly leaves and flowers of rich pure blue, lying like deep pools in hollows. *P. rubra* has coral-red flowers which never turn blue, followed by large rosettes of velvety light-green leaves.

Halfway along the Shady Walk, an old hawthorn tree was decapitated, the roots treated so that it would not grow again and the trunk then used as a support for ivy. Now *Hedera colchica* 'Sulphur Heart' (which we originally called 'Paddy's Pride'), a large-leaved ivy with irregular yellow centres to the leaves, forms a tall column with a rather dark holly as a good backdrop to it. By making use in this way of unwanted stumps, quick vertical interest can be obtained while waiting for newly planted trees to achieve height. From January onwards there will be a succession of snowdrops along this gently curving border. I am not yet an avid collector so I cannot say exactly how many different kinds I have – maybe thirty with interesting differences – but I have heard keen collectors talk about a hundred or more. There are a few rhododendrons along the boundary bank but this is not rhododendron country. If I could grow them easily I am sure I would be tempted to grow more, especially the wild unimproved species, which I much prefer. Many of those I have are forms of *Rhododendron ponticum*, valued primarily for their evergreen leaves and their wind resistance. If you are not so troubled by dessicating winds as I am, then you can grow many more beautiful ones.

There is room in this part of the garden for some of the more rampant ground-cover plants. One of the loveliest, in spring and early summer, is an American phlox, *Phlox stolonifera*. Above prostrate rosettes of light green stand heads of soft blue or white flowers. One of the best ground-cover plants in spring, although it is not exactly what I would choose, is the native celandine. If you have only a small garden it is possible, where it becomes a weed, to remove every piece, but here on such a big scale I find that a hopeless task. Anyway, it is very attractive early in the year, creating wide patches of yellow flowers among the strong perennials that have not yet emerged, and does not seem to harm them.

Viola labradorica is one of my favourite ground-cover plants; modest, with its small dark-purple leaves and light-purple flowers,

These strange spidery clumps of flat black leaves still find me searching for ways to show them off. Ophiopogon planiscapus nigrescens produces short sprays of small pink Lily of the Valley-like flowers tucked in among the strap-shaped leaves in early autumn, followed by shining black berries which remain throughout winter. With it I have planted a plum-purple form of Helleborus orientalis and Erythronium dens-canis with mauve flowers and chocolate-blotched leaves.

This bay between shrubs is at the lower end of the long shady walk. Here in spring it is colourful with daffodils and many species of Pulmonaria that have added to our confusion by interbreeding and producing hybrid offspring. They spend the summer building up these handsome basal leaf rosettes that still look good in October. Epimediums and Solomon's Seal make contrasting autumn tints. The evergreen to the right is the golden-leaved Yew, Taxus baccata 'Elegantissima', a glorious sight in early summer when every new shoot is bright yellow. Offering pale yellow leaves all summer and autumn is Weigela 'Looymansii Aurea', which appreciates this partially shaded site.

Making a good foreground here are robust clumps of a double white primrose I grew originally from seed. It does not have quite the charm of the very old and delicate Primula vulgaris 'Alba Plena' but is so much healthier and easier to grow. I have tried many old double primroses, including P. v. 'Lilacina', but they do not like my soil and are martyrs to pests like the Red Spider Mite.

Left: an example of the close carpeting of soil in shady areas beneath trees and shrubs. It is early March. Snowdrop foliage can just be seen becoming buried among the fast-moving herbage. The little blue-mauve Corydalis solida is just flowering – it needs to be planted in drifts to be effective – and comes and goes as quickly as the wood anemones. Beside it is a leaf rosette of the white-flowered foxglove, Digitalis purpurea 'Alba'. It is easy to tell at this stage if the flowers will be white: the leaf-stalks will be green at the base (they will be stained purple if the flowers are to be purple). Aquilegias have seeded around and will flower before the foxgloves. Arum italicum 'Pictum' leaves make contrast and indicate that there will be a show of red berries here in the autumn.

it comes true from seed, and spreads adventitiously, running round hostas and other heavy clumps. It has no scent. Only *V. odorata* is scented, with purple, white or pink flowers but I find it more difficult to grow than the other violets; its leaves are so often attacked by aphids, I believe, or some pest which causes the leaves to thicken and roll up in an unsightly fashion.

Invaluable as ground cover in large shrubberies are *Trachystemon orientale* and *Pachysandra terminalis*, but both are very invasive plants. *Helleborus foetidus* and *Chrysanthemum parthenium* 'Aureum' provide shade and cover around the leaves of a special dwarf narcissus in summer. There will also be shade from the oak overhead, all helping to keep away the dreaded Narcissus Fly which likes to lay its eggs in the neck of the bulb.

Another handsome but rampant scrambler is *Rubus tricolor*. I use it as cover either under trees or falling down a bank. I have also seen it grown up a fence. It is a relative of the bramble, but why it is called '*tricolor*' I cannot think as it seems to me to have only two colours. It makes trails of long, lax stems covered with soft copper-coloured bristles. Simple shining leaves eventually make extensive ground cover in shade, even over birch roots. I think it might get damaged in very cold areas – it has been damaged here in very severe winters.

Because there is so much work to be done one does not always notice what is happening and does not cut back in time something which is becoming too invasive. An attractive yellow-leaved ivy has taken over too much ground at one end of the Long Shady Walk and there are erythroniums underneath which could be choked. Certainly the silver-leaved *Lamium maculatum* is being squeezed out, so I must make time to sort out all these invaders.

This simple picture (below) gives me much pleasure, capturing one of the fleeting designs of autumn. The leaves of a cherry, Prunus sargentii, have fallen on to the silver-leaved Pulmonaria saccharata 'Argentea'. The cherry makes a tall upright tree, breathtaking for a week or so in spring when single pink flowers hang among freshly unfolded leaves tinted reddish-bronze. In autumn if you make the effort to seek it out, you will gaze spellbound at the sight of fiery-red and apricot leaves held high against a blue sky. All too soon they fall overnight forming a half circle over the mown grass, creating a pattern like this that could perhaps suggest ideas for fabric designs.

HOSTA

H. crispula
This is similar to 'Thomas Hogg' (discussed overleaf) but has larger, darker green leaves with undulating edges broadly banded with white. It prefers to be grown in shade. 75cm/2½ft. Zone 5.

H. fortunei 'Albo Picta'
A great garden favourite, it does best in deep moist soil in shade. The leaves alone will then be up to 23cm/9in long and 15cm/6in across with a delicate, almost translucent texture. They are variegated when they first open with a yellow and cream centre and a border of dark green. The leaf becomes completely green by midsummer. 75cm/2½ft. Zone 5.

H. fortunei 'Aurea'
Its delicate leaves are completely butter-yellow at first but turn light green by summer. 45cm/1½ft. Zone 5.

Most of the hostas grown in gardens are hybrids or sports. Some originally came from Japanese garden clones, others are still being introduced by hybridizers in America and Japan. While some hostas will do fairly well in drier situations if the soil is enriched with humus and covered with a mulch, they all perform much better in moist soil in part shade. The yellow-leaved forms in particular need shelter from direct sunlight, which can scorch their thin leaves, although they do need indirect light so their leaves do not turn green too quickly. The 'blue'-leaved forms – dark-green leaves covered with a waxy bloom – grow much better in part shade. The uncharacteristic wet summers of the past two years have damaged my blue-leaved hostas, apparently destroying the protective wax coating, causing the leaf edges to curl and go brown. Once planted in suitable conditions, hostas should not be disturbed.

Hostas do attract snails and slugs but I try not to use slug bait harmful to other forms of life, including predatory beetles as well as birds. The rough texture of pulverized bark helps to deter them.

All hostas can be planted in containers or tubs provided they are sheltered from strong sunlight and kept well fed and watered. The following forms (the variegated ones are shown overleaf) are well known in gardens.

H. fortunei 'Marginato-Alba'
The moderately large and heavily corrugated leaves are sage-green and ivory and in rich soil will produce very dramatic variegations if sufficiently shaded. 75cm/2½ft. Zone 5.

H. fortunei 'Obscura Marginata' (*H.* 'Gold Edge')
Sometimes mistakenly called H.f. 'Marginata Aurea', this is an excellent garden plant that will take more light than most of the hostas, provided the soil is not too dry. Similar to H. ventricosa 'Variegata' (overleaf) but with larger, more rounded leaves that are broader at the base. A broad irregular greenish-yellow edge surrounds a slightly puckered, dark rich-green centre. The variegation lasts well into autumn. It quickly forms a good-sized clump. 60cm/2ft. Zone 5.

H. fortunei 'Aurea'

H. 'T F × 22'

H. tardiana 'Halcyon'

H. 'Honeybells'
Descended from H. planta-
ginea (opposite), it has in-
herited some of its perfume
but has very pale lilac flow-
ers. The leaves are similar –
light olive-green and pointed
with undulating edges – but
stronger, remaining fresh
and healthy when some
hostas are past their best.
90cm/3ft. Zone 5.

H. 'Krossa Regal'
This is a large, grey-leaved
plant. Handsome glaucous
leaves on tall stems are
lightly corrugated with
parallel veins. Each tip tilts
upwards so the wavy edges
show a glimpse of pale grey
blue bloom on the under-

H. 'Royal Standard'

side. It produces spires of
lilac flowers in mid- to late
summer. 90–120cm/3–4ft.
Zone 5.

H. lancifolia
Although smaller and plain-
er than the others, it has
attractive narrow, shiny
dark green leaves which
form overlapping mounds,
making this plant useful as a
ground cover. Large, deep-
lilac trumpets on tall slen-
der stems give a long display
in late summer. 90cm/3ft.
Zone 5.

H. plantaginea
This rare plant is not the
easiest to grow. It needs
moisture and warmth well

into the autumn. Then, in October, it produces very large, deliciously scented lily-like flowers with the colour and texture of white marble. The leaves too are beautiful – arching heart-shapes of a glossy yellowish-green. 60cm/2ft. Zone 7.

H. 'Royal Standard'
A valued hybrid, more robust and generously flowering than its parent H. plantaginea. 60cm/2ft. Zone 5.

H. sieboldiana
Has the largest, most dramatic leaves of all the hostas – in ideal conditions up to 45cm/1½ft long and 30cm/1ft across. Just above the mounds of grey-blue leaves, the pale lilac flowers stand on stumpy heads. In autumn, after the first frost, the foliage colour turns to glowing shades of honey. 75cm/2½ft. Zone 5.

H. sieboldiana 'Elegans'
This is a selected form with very large leaves in a deeper grey-blue tone, deeply veined and puckered. 75cm/2½ft. Zone 5.

H. 'T F × 22'
I still list this hosta under the number given it by its breeder, Eric Smith. I value it for the dense clusters of small, overlapping blue leaves. 30cm/12in. Zone 5.

H. tardiana 'Halcyon'
This is possibly the best blue-leaved Hosta. In my garden it holds its blue colouring longer than other blue-leaved hostas. Fine heads of lilac-blue flowers are held on purplish stems in late summer. 30cm/1ft. Zone 5.

H. fortunei 'Albo Picta' (with *H. univittata* in the foreground)

H. fortunei 'Marginato Alba'

H. fortunei 'Obscura Marginata'

H. 'Yellow Splash'

H. 'Thomas Hogg'
This reliable Hosta, though not as glamorous as some, is never untidy or boring. Its smooth-textured, medium-sized green leaves are narrow with pointed tips and wavy white margins extending partly down the leaf-stalk. The centre of the leaf is shaded in light and dark green. 60cm/2ft. Zone 5.

H. ventricosa
With broad heart-shaped, evenly veined, rich dark-green foliage, this is the finest of the green-leaved hostas. Apart from H. plantaginea, it has the finest flowers too – large deep-lilac bells, more rounded and with veining inside. 60cm/2ft. Zone 5.

H. ventricosa 'Variegata'
The leaf has a butter-yellow border which seeps into its centre. It is not the most vigorous of hostas and needs patience, good conditions, moisture and feeding. 60cm/2ft. Zone 5.

H. 'Yellow Splash'
This hybrid has narrow, brightly variegated leaves, the vivid colouring continuing until autumn frosts. This hosta will tolerate open conditions better than some variegated ones. 30cm/1ft. Zone 5.

The Dry Garden

A sudden chilling shower has folded the petals of Anemone fulgens *which grows wild in Greece and Turkey, in open places, in sun-baked sandy soil. The intensely scarlet flowers are filled with navy-blue stamens and contrast well with the whorled, blue-green-leaved stems of* Euphorbia wulfenii, *but are even more exciting seen on a hot sunny day beside the vivid lime-green heads of* E. polychroma.

This view shows part of the Mediterranean Garden in midsummer. Yellow is one of the dominant colours at this time of year, seen here in this Mount Etna Broom, Genista aetnensis, *whose sweet scent drenches the garden on warm still days. Below it the foliage of* Melissa officinalis 'Aurea' *continues the yellow theme, and so do the flowers of one of the shrubby potentillas, but a monochrome would be very dull. Here also are soft pinks of* Alstroemeria ligtu *hybrids, orange lilies, white campions and plenty of soft grey foliage to buffer any dis-quieting colour mixtures.*

IT IS HARD looking at this part of the garden today to imagine just what it was like thirty years ago. Very little grew on it, as the soil was so poor and dry that even the native weeds curled up and died in long weeks of drought. This part of the land – around the south-west facing side of the house – consisted of almost pure gravel, with scarcely any dark humus soil on top, so we knew that we would have problems in most dry summers. In 1960 we moved into the newly built house and I sat on a south-facing slope in the sun, dug my hand into the warm bank and brought out white sand – it ran through my fingers like sand in an egg-timer. Although I thought we understood something about drought-resistant plants, having always lived in this part of the country where it is particularly dry, I knew this was going to be drier than anything we had ever had before. Our first garden in Colchester had been based on chalky boulder clay, which is more retentive and does not dry out quite so quickly.

To start with I collected all the leaf-mould I could find around the place, which was not much, and then I bought mushroom compost which was a great help (it contains a fairly high proportion of chalk, so you must be careful where you put it if you wish to grow lime-hating plants like rhododendrons, certain primulas, and other plants from damp woodland conditions). I began with the premise that I would have a problem with drought however much organic matter I used because of the very low rainfall and because the soil was so free-draining. I knew that even if I managed to improve the texture of the soil with organic matter that would hold some moisture for a while, the planting had to depend largely on species adapted by nature to drought. I thought immediately of grey-leaved foliage plants like *Cerastium*, silver filigree-leaved artemisias, bush sages and handsome waxy-leaved euphorbias, all from sunny, stony areas around the Mediterranean. Hence my two

Eryngium giganteum

Eryngium tripartitum (of gardens)
Wiry, wide-spreading branching stems carry many cone-shaped heads surrounded by deeper blue spiny bracts in midsummer. 45cm/1½ft. Zone 6.

E. variifolium
Forms a flat handsome rosette of green richly marbled leaves with heads of small spiky flowers in late summer. The small spiny leaves ascending the stems and the flowers themselves

are so stiff that the whole effect is metallic. 45cm/ 1½ft. Zone 6.

Onopordum acanthium
Commonly called the Scotch Thistle. A splendid feature plant that forms a rosette of

huge spiny leaves copiously felted with white down. The towering flower-stem is topped with pale-lilac thistle flowers from midsummer to autumn. Needs sun and good drainage. 2m/6ft. Zone 4.

Over the years the shape of this small Mediterranean Garden has changed as I have been able to afford to buy more compost and materials to make raised beds. Some of the beds are raised to different levels, which I think adds to the design of the garden. If you have a flat garden, and a small one in particular, you can change it and improve it out of all recognition by making raised beds. They need only be raised knee-high or so, or even less – just 15cm/6in sometimes will do. If you can acquire enough soil, and add well-made compost or old farmyard manure and grit to im-

About half-way down this stepped gravel path is the place where, in 1960, I sat and trickled dry sandy soil through my fingers, wondering if it could ever become furnished with plants. This picture, taken in October, shows in the foreground part of the Mediterranean Garden as it looks all winter, covered with ever-grey or evergreen foliage while it waits to provide changing colour schemes of flowers throughout the next growing season. In late autumn pink lily-like flowers of Nerine bowdenii *and the floating moth-like white flowers of* Gaura lindheimeri *add soft colour to the quiet scene. Upright columnar yews make strong verticals against the horizontal edges of the steps, which have ramped fronts so that the barrows can be more easily pushed up and down them.*

prove the quality and create the required depth, it is very helpful.

Along the west-facing wall which separates the garden from the nursery there is now a raised bed about 45cm/18in high. There, in the original border of poor sandy soil, even the native weeds curled up and died, and the sedums and sempervivums shrank to their innermost rosettes. The soil sometimes felt warm enough to poach an egg on it during some of the summers we have had.

To start with, we raised the surface by adding a mixture of improved soil, grit and compost. A peat bed would be totally unsuitable and impossible to maintain in such a dry situation. Good drainage was provided because none of these plants would tolerate too much wet at their roots. When the bed was finally planted, it was mulched with grit. This helps to keep weeds down, but – most important – makes nice dry collars for plants to rest on, so they will not rot off at the necks. Many of the plants here are from rock slides or gritty scree areas. When you see them growing wild in the mountains, it is only too easy to be misled. Your back and your nose may well be scorching, and the rocks so hot that you cannot bear to sit on them, but you see these lovely little cushion plants studding the ground and you think, 'That would look lovely in my East Anglian garden.' Not a bit of it. Although the plants are hot on the surface, underneath they are being fed by melting snow from perhaps 300m/1,000ft away which is trickling down.

I am not attempting to grow such plants, which are the delight of alpine enthusiasts, but what I am able to grow are plants which thrive in the mountains around the Mediterranean – ones like *Dianthus*, *Sedum* and *Sempervivum* that will endure drier conditions and spend the summer sitting on parched stony soil.

DESIGNING THE PLANTING

Most people accept that they will put their small plants at the front and their large plants at the back. This is a very good principle, but can be boring if adhered to rigidly. I think to have the occasional plant which breaks that habit and comes forward as a mound or even a small vertical on the front edge of the bed creates an element of surprise, rather than the inevitable flat mat. To depart from these basic principles occasionally gives a much more lively effect. The other principle I use in planting is based on the asymmetric triangle. This is difficult to explain but easy to understand when you see it (see page 17). Looking at it in profile, we pass through tiny-leaved, sweetly scented thymes, and groups of low-growing euphorbias, through larger mounds of silvery-grey lavender and *Ballota*, to *Euphorbia wulfenii*, which is taller still, until we meet a little Judas tree (*Cercis siliquastrum*), which is not very tall yet. But the eye has been lifted as the line leads up to the sky, to the *Cupressus arizonica* beyond, a useful drought-loving coniferous tree. The skyline does not look as though the plants had been pushed in like walking-sticks in a hallstand. They carry a profile. This may not happen everywhere, but where it does, and where two triangles meet sometimes, I find it makes an effective frame for the view beyond. I use this principle with even a small group of plants. I may plant a tall feathery fennel. Beside the fennel might be the shrub *Phlomis fruticosa*, a bulky rounded shape. As strong

Graptopetalum paraguayense

Kleinia vitalis

Crassula argentea

Mediterranean plants (above) form a comfortable colourful group in early summer. Fresh filigree grey foliage on Santolina chamaecyparis needs the contrast of large simple leaves like those of Verbascum pulverulentum whose almost white felted leaves can form flower-like rosettes more than 60cm/2ft across, while the candelabra-like flower-heads can reach heights of up to 2.3m/8ft. Perfect contrast among these ashen groups is the electric-green of Euphorbia wulfenii.

Artemisia canescens (left) is one of the most beautiful of grey plants. From a low twiggy base the new season's growth forms a forest of slender wiry stems each carrying finely divided wisps of foliage. As summer drought intensifies, the plants become silvery-white, standing out as a feature when all flowers have faded.

The focal point in this picture is the almost white foliage and flower-heads of Stachys olympica 'Cotton Boll'. Behind, repeating the vertical lines, are the flowering stems of Ballota acetabulosa. Beyond, to the left, can be seen the yellow variegated leaves of Melissa officinalis 'Variegata' and the glaucous blue of Ruta graveolens 'Jackman's Blue'.

This picture (right) shows one of the hybrid pinks as part of a group where both the colour of the flowers and the colour and shape of its foliage will add to the overall effect. Artemisia 'Powis Castle' forms the largest and most imposing plant in the background. To the left Anaphalis triplinervis forms clusters of small smooth grey leaves when waiting to produce sprays of tiny everlasting daisies in early autumn. Between them all runs a stream of Thymus 'Golden Carpet', at its brightest and best in winter.

Above: one of a number of named and unnamed small hybrid pinks we grow in the mixed groups of low-growing plants along the edges of sunny well-drained borders. There are both single and double forms. They flower for weeks in midsummer, often producing odd flowers late in the autumn. Many are scented. I value them also for their neat cushions of blue-grey leaves, usually smaller and more dense than some of the larger hybrid pinks.

contrast in form you might use a spiky-leaved *Yucca* nearby and then the eye will travel down to low mounds of *Ballota* or *Santolina*, and finally descend to the mat plants. Together they form a related group. If you can compose individual groups linked together within the external frame it makes the planting look much more interesting both overall and in detail. You will find you have little bays, or low places, separated by larger plants which in some places will come right forward to the edge of the planting. To have a 'hedge' along the back of tall plants, all of the same height, solid like a row of bookcases, and all the flat cushions along the front, is very uninteresting. Stick to the general principle – have smallish things at the front, big things at the back – but bear in mind that if you plant them in groups some of those bigger things will come towards the front and make a more attractive irregular edge.

FOLIAGE

It is a never-ending pleasure making patterns with leaves, regardless of the flowers. In this garden even in November, when there is not a flower in sight, there is still plenty of colour with silver and grey, grey-blue and glaucous green. Bronze tangles of shrubby potentillas add warmth. There is still a lot of colour without flowers. Just as interesting are the many forms and textures, with

Left: part of the stepped path leading from the hot dry garden to one of the shade gardens sheltered by the big oak and holly. Narrow spires of Verbascum chaixii *break the low line and 'bun' shapes of surrounding plants, as does the greyish-white delphinium growing in a cooler situation in the background. The soft lemon-yellow of* Anthemis tinctoria *'E.C. Buxton' is repeated in this unusual perennial nasturtium,* Tropaeolum polyphyllum, *whose writhing trails can be seen creeping out over the surface of the step. The small poppies in the foreground were bred by the late Sir Cedric Morris who took the red poppy of the cornfields and spent half a lifetime selecting, in his attempt to produce a blue one. He did not succeed entirely but the strain he achieved (now offered sometimes as* Papaver *'Fairy Wings') comes in shades of soft lilac, greyish-purple and sometimes in white with crimson rims.*

Phlox douglasii, *which can be found in shades of pink, white or blue, makes a dense low mound of firm, finely cut foliage that will eventually hang like a shawl over a low wall, masking the hard edge.*

This view (left), taken in midsummer, is the part of the Mediterranean Garden we see from the office window, or from the back entrance to the house. The free-draining gravel supports a rich tapestry of flowers and foliage. Reminiscent of pointilliste *paintings, most of the flowers appear as small vivid dots of colour against a background of predominantly grey foliage.*

EUPHORBIA

There are many species of *Euphorbia*, some of which have become very popular both in gardens and as cut flowers. The fresh lime-green peculiar to euphorbias illuminates the garden from March to September. Some, from warm Mediterranean areas, are suited to dry conditions and well-drained soil. A few from woodlands prefer cool shady places, while one at least is adapted to damp soil. In size they vary from a sprawling, starfish shape to a plant taking the place of a shrub, several feet tall and across.

E. griffithii 'Fireglow'
Has tomato-red flowers, light olive foliage with red veins and orange-brown stems. It will grow in full sun and likes retentive soil. There is a darker-flowered form called E.g. 'Dixter'. The veins and backs of the young leaves are coral-red and the flowers a brilliant flame-red. The chaplet of leaflets beneath the flower cluster is also stained with this bright colour. It flowers from early to late summer. 90–120cm/3–4ft. Zone 6.

E. longifolia
Handsome for weeks in mid-summer. Begins with a closely packed small head of vivid lime flowers set off by white-veined leaves. Side branches appear, carrying more flowers until a large loose head is formed. Several stems arise from one root-stock. Needs rich retentive soil in part shade. 90cm/3ft. Zone 6.

E. myrsinites
Prostrate stems radiate from a central point carrying wax-coated blue leaves and terminating in a large head of lime-green apricot-tinged flowers in early spring. 15cm/6in. Zone 5.

E. palustris
Its many leafy stems create a bushy shape up to several feet across. It is topped with wide flat heads of greenish-gold flowers for several weeks in spring and early summer. Odd fresh flowers appear later in the year and in the autumn the dying foliage sometimes turns to brilliant shades of cream, orange and crimson. Needs moist soil. 90–120cm/3–4ft. Zone 6.

E. pilosa 'Major'
In spring looks like a larger form of E. polychroma but the foliage is more luxuriant. Produces a late crop of autumn flowers. 45cm/1½ft. Zone 6.

E. polychroma (epithymoides)
One of the best with neat mounds of brassy-yellow heads all spring. The whole plant takes on coral tints in autumn. 38cm/15in. Zone 5.

E. robbiae
Although it will grow in dry shade, this evergreen spurge is marvellous in good retentive soil. It is invasive, so is not suitable for very small gardens. Handsome dark green rosettes carry showy heads of yellowish-green flowers which open in spring and last through most of the summer, turning bronze-tinted in autumn. Useful as evergreen ground cover. 60–75cm/2–2½ft. Zone 6.

E. seguieriana (E. s. niciciana)
A superb plant. Following E. polychroma, it blooms for three months, with exquisite lime-green flower-heads on many thin stems. The leaves are narrow and blue-grey. 45cm/1½ft. Zone 6.

Mixed hybrids between **E. wulfenii** and **E. characias**

E. myrsinites

E. sikkimensis
In February and March basal rosettes of ruby-red leaves appear at ground level. Quickly the stems elongate, becoming tall and willowy, and the leaves become light green with a white vein and red leaf-stalks, giving a very fresh effect from the end of July into September. Flowering begins in early July and by August the round blue-green seed-pods contrast with vivid lime-green collars. The central head is surrounded by two or three side branches which carry fresh flowers in autumn. 1.2–1.5m/4–5ft. Zone 6.

E. wulfenii
A dramatic feature plant in the dry garden. Handsome all the year round. Long stiff stems clothed in blue-grey foliage form a large clump. From March to May each stem carries a huge head of lime-green flowers. Likes shelter from wind. E. characias is the Mediterranean form, a tougher plant whose dull green flowers have sinister-looking black eyes. These two forms are much interbred in gardens and often cannot be named with any certainty. 90–120cm/3–4ft. Zone 6.

E. polychroma

very feathery leaves and larger simpler leaves which you must have for contrast. If the overall design is fussy, made with only tiny leaves like those of thyme and lavender, there is no impact. So what gives the impact here? *Euphorbia wulfenii*, and in the background, the fine bright sword-shaped leaves of *Iris foetidissima*. *Ballota* is another good contrast plant, with its mounds of felty, almost suede-like white leaves. If we have a really severe winter we may lose most of the top growth, but it always comes back again from the base. Quite a different colour and texture is added with the blue-green filigree leaves of *Ruta graveolens* 'Jackman's Blue', but you have to be careful how you handle Rue. I am very allergic to it, as I am now to many of the plants in the garden, but the problem didn't begin until I was in my forties. It may have resulted from over-exposure.

When all the flowers have gone, and some of the foliage too, there is still enough shape to make you feel that the garden is furnished in winter. More than any other part, the dry garden remains interesting all year round.

In the summer, the Mediterranean Garden is wonderfully scented. Why the Lord decided to put perfume into these leaves, goodness knows, but I think aromatic oils are a way of conserving moisture and keeping the leaf active in very dry conditions. There are thymes here which smell of caraway seeds and of lemon. Even in winter there is still an odd leaf on the Lemon Verbena (*Lippia*

In July regal lilies (Lilium regale – below) stand among the soaring stems of the Wild Leek (Allium ampeloprasum), whose opening flowers are disappearing out of the top of the picture (see also page 148). Verbascum chaixii 'Album' forms subsidiary verticals in the background while the tiny green-flowered umbellifer, Bupleurum falcatum will continue to flower for weeks throughout late summer, forming a cloud of yellowish-green and enhancing its neighbours.

The appeal of this picture lies, I think, in the lemon-yellow foliage of Melissa officinalis 'Aurea'. Above it stand tall stems of Allium bulgaricum bearing alabaster-like flowers. One stem just opening is about to release its pointed envelope before the bells droop down in cowslip fashion. Soft orange, semi-double poppies, Papaver rupifragum, have crumpled tissue-paper-like petals. Lilium 'Viking' stands waiting its turn to steal the scene. The evergreen strap-shaped leaves of Iris foetidissima furnish this corner in winter when all the rest have gone.

142

Against the dark screen of a Leylandii hedge stiff stems of Papaver orientale *'Beauty of Livermore' make an interesting pattern. The large, mostly unopened bristly buds, clasped by leafy bracts, indicate one of the parents must not have had this characteristic, as can be seen by another hybrid in the foreground.*

citriodora) with its wonderfully fresh lemon scent under the south wall of the house, and the Lemon Balm at its feet is also scented.

Among the tall plants I like to use is *Verbascum pulverulentum* – it provides another dramatic leaf for the Mediterranean area. This tall yellow-flowered Mullein, and the Giant Thistle (*Onopordum acanthium*), are both excellent architectural plants, which I have used to give height to this part of the garden while waiting for the permanent trees to grow. Several forms of *Acanthus* have tall stately flower-heads, but you must be careful where you put *Acanthus* because it is one of those plants you can grow from root cuttings, so every bit left in the ground will try to make a new plant. Where I have made a mistake I have had to give up trying to move it. Nothing short of weedkiller will destroy it. All the forms have spectacular foliage, from the bold curving shape of *A. mollis* to the almost hedgehog-like prickliness of *A. spinosissima*.

I try to avoid talking about any plants as favourites, because every plant has an important role to play and so much depends on where and how you plant, but *Euphorbia wulfenii* is a most beautiful plant. Its blue-green leaves really stand out as something exceptional, especially in winter. Although it can be found wild south of the Massif Central and throughout the southern Mediterranean, it will stand severe winters without shelter. I have never lost it completely here in thirty years. There are always seedlings to be found, and in two years, you can have a good-sized plant back again. In the southern half of the country, and especially in well-drained soil, it presents no problem in most winters.

Although I have talked a lot about the 'furniture' of the dry garden – the basic background plants, what I call the armchairs, sideboards, and carpets – you also need those personal little

Seen from the top of a shallow flight of steps this pot garden is one which decorates the sitting room terrace. The striking purple rosettes in the centre belong to Aeonicum arboretum *'Atropurpureum' while other succulents, species of* Cotyledon, Echeveria *and others, add striking changes of texture and form to the frothy bouquets of* Pelargonium *and* Helichrysum petiolare. *Large pots of* Chrysanthemum frutescens *'Paris White', purple-leaved cannas, cordylines and variegated forms of* Agave americana *all add to the exotic-looking combination of flowers and good leaves.*

objects that you collect – the lamps, pictures and pieces of china that put character into a room. So it is in a garden. You can begin in spring with bulbs – the small bulbs like crocuses, chionodoxas and bulbous iris. Very poor gravel soil is usually too dry for daffodils to do well except for some of the wild Spanish forms like *Narcissus triandrus* 'Angel's Tears' and *N. asteriensis* (*minimus*). Being small and with delicate flowers, they fit in far better with the low mats of thyme or *Artemisia* than the big blowsy blooms of some of the cultivated and 'improved' *Narcissus*.

The main season of large bulbs in this part of the garden starts with alliums in late April or May. There are several species here including *Allium bulgaricum*, *A. aflatunense* and *A. christophii*. They stand well above the foliage of the other plants, making a great effect. They are such good value in the garden because they carry the bulb season from spring to autumn, making attractive drifts of mauve, white and pink long after other spring bulbs have vanished. Lilies do well here, too. Throughout June, July and August there is a succession of different varieties and species. Other good verticals are the starry white flowers of *Asphodelus albus* in June, while the Yellow Asphodel (*Asphodeline liburnica*), continues into late summer. I like to see them placed in a void

This view is part of the little paved yard outside my office window and the back door of the house. Pots of pelargoniums (the old French varieties of ivy-leaved geranium) with Helichrysum petiolare, *scarlet trumpets of* Vallota purpurea *and various succulents are grouped together on different levels, using concrete blocks to make removable platforms. By the end of summer the containers (whether handsome terracotta pots or plain black plastic buckets) become hidden in the enveloping trails of foliage and flower.*

where they are not pressed close up against something else.

Mound-shaped plants like lavender, *Santolina*, *Ballota* and Rue can look like buns in a baking tray if you do not have vertical spires and grasses planted among them. There are lovely grasses for the dry garden. *Stipa gigantea* is superb with its shimmering heads of golden oat-like flowers held high on 2m/6ft stems.

Plants with iris-like leaves like *Libertia* and *Sisyrinchium* offer much-needed vertical shapes. Autumn ends with the delicate rosy-pink trumpets of *Nerine bowdenii* and the silk-textured flowers of *Schizostylis coccinea* (also known as Kaffir Lilies), but these end-of-season plants can be awkward to place. They come from South Africa and do not flower until late autumn – lasting into December if the weather is mild. They must have real warmth during the summer to bring them into flower, plus sufficient moisture to make good plants.

Another of my star performers – in part of the dry garden going down towards the water-garden – is *Gaura lindheimeri*. These delicate-looking plants disappear in winter but mercifully come back in spring to form upright branching stems simply smothered later in the year with little pink-flushed white flowers. In the dusk of summer evenings they look like clouds of moths. They flower from June to November and even in a mild January there is a flower good enough to remind you what the plant was like.

As you walk down the slope from the dry garden, you pass through the dry gravel at the upper level into another grade of soil. We call it silt: it is much denser than sand but not as dense as clay. It is black and looks as if it would grow absolutely anything and everything. In actual fact, I found that it would not, because it is so close-textured that many plants cannot penetrate it. Their roots stay in the top inch or two. So the texture of the soil had to be improved. It did not need a lot of additional humus, but we dug in plenty of grit and small stones to aerate it, and to allow rain to penetrate, because when this kind of soil is totally dry, the rain runs off the surface, especially on a slope. Here I am able to grow plants which do not need wet soil but must have a retentive one.

This whole area is in the process of being completely changed but there are plants like the tree heathers *Erica arborea* and *E. lusitanica* and a few dwarf rhododendrons which will be retained, but I must now think of groupings of plants that will create a garden of different character from any we have elsewhere.

ALLIUM

A. aflatunense
Has flower-heads the size of small oranges, packed with deep-lilac flowers in May, carried on tall slender stems. 90–120cm/3–4ft. Zone 7.

A. ampeloprasum
The Wild Leek's large spherical buds burst open to form dense heads of small pink flowers. 1.5–1.8m/ 5–6ft. Zone 6.

A. ampeloprasum
A. christophii (top)

These ornamental onions include a great variety of shapes and sizes, and carry the bulb season forward into the summer months, making drifts of colour long after other spring bulbs have finished flowering.

Most of the alliums will grow in poor soil, but do much better if fed with well-rotted manure or compost. Some tend to over-produce themselves, scattering their seeds into everything around them and making bulbils in their flower-heads, while under the soil the main bulb proliferates into millions of bulblets. These I avoid, but listed here are a few of those that I value in the garden. Many of them have the additional attraction of eye-catching seed-heads later in the year. (The seed-heads are also valuable for flower arrangements.)

A. aflatunense (with **Armeria** 'Düsseldorf Pride') (top)

A. atropurpurcum
Upturned clusters of dark purple flowers in June. 60cm/2ft. Zone 6.

A. cernuum
Looks very attractive growing out of a carpet of thyme when graceful stems carry elegant nodding heads of little deep-amethyst flowers. 45cm/1½ft. Zone 6.

A. christophii (albopilosum)
This plant, both strong and delicate, has amazing globular flower-heads the size of small footballs. Each is made of many metallic-looking lilac stars in which the petals touch tip to tip. It dries well, the delicate spoke-like stems retaining their purple colour. 60cm/2ft. Zone 7.

A. flavum
This small plant is distinguished by its tight little clumps of almost blue foliage set off by heads of small lemon-yellow bells in mid- to late summer. 23cm/9in. Zone 6.

A. karataviense
In early spring the leaves emerge tightly rolled, showing their maroon edges. They open broad and curving, a dark pewter-green, setting off the pale beige-pink head, large as a tennis ball, between them. When the leaves disappear, the fleshy seed capsules dry into translucent petals. 15cm/6in. Zone 6.

A. nigrum
Found wild in SE Europe. It has densely packed flattish heads of purple flowers but it varies in depth of colour. 90cm/3ft. Zone 7.

A. siculum dioscorides (seed-heads)

A. oreophilum
This short-stemmed Allium looks best broadcast in small groups on the edges of dry sunny borders. In mid-summer it produces small clustered heads of large deep-rose-pink flowers, which dry into sun-bleached pale papery seed-heads. 10cm/4in. Zone 7.

A. pulchellum
In July and August this dainty Allium sends up a number of slender stems from which dangle masses of dusty-lilac bells. 38cm/15in. Zone 7.

A. pulchellum 'Album'
An exquisite white form that holds its flowers in tall pointed cases before they split open. 30–60cm/12–24in. Zone 7.

A. schubertii
Makes heads equally large as, and sometimes larger than, A. christophii, but each head has flowers arranged on different lengths of stem, so creating a recessed effect. Individual stems are thick and the seed capsules large so the whole head dries to a more robust-looking form as though carved from wood. Unfortunately it starts into growth early in spring and is often caught and killed by late frosts. 60–75cm/2–2½ft. Zone 7.

A. senescens (montanum)
In late summer cool lilac heads are held above flat vigorous clumps of swirling grey-green leaves. 15cm/6in. Zone 7.

A. siculum
Possibly the most handsome allium. Tall, thick stems are topped with flowers encased in papery pointed envelopes. When these split, they reveal dangling heads of large open bells, creamy-green flushed with purple. 90cm/3ft. Zone 7.

A. siculum dioscorides (A.s. bulgaricum)
Very similar to the above but the waxen bells are plum-coloured. In both, the drooping bell-like flowers, once fertilized, return to an upright position, each seed capsule topped with a pointed cap. 90cm/3ft. Zone 6.

A. sphaerocephalum
The small bulbs divide freely so can quickly produce a mass of slender bare stems topped with small plum-shaped heads of purple flowers in late summer. 45cm/1½ft. Zone 7.

A. atropurpureum

A. nigrum

The Reservoir Garden

THIS PART of the garden is an open area of large informal borders with wide grassy walks. Although the soil here can dry out after a long period without rain, it is not as poor as in the Mediterranean Garden. We added a layer of clay to the original gravel soil when we dredged the reservoir and spread it when dry like caked face powder over the gravel. Trees and shrubs have done well in the centres of these beds, their strong roots able to cope with the stiff surface clay, while a regular straw mulch is improving the topsoil layer. But I had to remove some of the clay from the wider borders around the shrubs, replace it with gravelly soil and then fork both soils together before adding more grit, compost and old farmyard manure to make an acceptable soil for herbaceous plants.

Whereas on the original gravel we had been restricted in our choice of plants, we are now able to grow, among others, some of the old border chrysanthemums, such as 'Anastasia' and 'Emperor of China'. The latter, an old hybrid chrysanthemum which was re-introduced by Graham Stuart Thomas, flowers in late autumn. Its beautifully quilled petals are deep crimson in the centre, fading to silvery white as the layers of petals unroll. There are several forms of *Chrysanthemum rubellum*, all very free-flowering with single flowers. *C.r.* 'Clara Curtis' makes stiff bushy plants completely smothered with rich-pink yellow-eyed daisies.

Some late-flowering salvias also enjoy this warm, south-facing site. They need the improved soil and would probably dry out in the driest of gravels. Among them are *Salvia ambigens* and S. *uliginosa*. The latter is a breathtaking sight in September, standing 120–150cm/4–5ft tall, each leafy stem topped with loose spires of sky-blue flowers. S. *ambigens* does not flower so freely, but its deep gentian-blue catches the eye. These plants are a little tender so they have to be covered with plant remains or bark in winter.

Cynara
cardunculus

Salvia
officinalis
'Icterina'

Stachys
olympica

Potentilla argyrophylla

Some of the hardy geraniums or cranesbills that do not like very gravelly soil also flourish here. One of them, *Geranium wallichianum* 'Buxton's Variety', is a treasure, producing royal-blue flowers, white-eyed and appealing, for weeks on end from late summer until the first frosts. Along the border edges I have planted the dwarf mountain forms of *Phlox* – *P. douglasii* and *P. serrulata*, which do well in these conditions – but not the tall border phloxes. They need a moister soil.

Most of the beds in the Reservoir Garden are what are termed 'island beds', being surrounded by mown grass. I always design mine with a spine of trees and shrubs. Sometimes the spine goes roughly through the middle of the bed, sometimes it may be offset to leave more space on one side or the other to make better use of the sunny or the shady side, as I mentioned in the Shade chapter.

Where I have a wide sunny side and a much narrower bed on the shady side, I consider the narrow side the 'minus' side because although it has seasonal interest it is not exciting all the year round. You walk past it rather than stop to enjoy individual treasures. Bold clumps of bergenias, hellebores and carpeting plants like lamiums and *Geranium maculatum* keep the soil free of weeds. In some places I feel there cannot be two borders of equal interest facing each other because we cannot absorb, let alone enjoy, too much at once. I think sometimes a quiet, unexciting piece of planting makes a necessary contribution to the design.

In a slight hollow I decided to allow more space for plants needing a protected shady environment. This enabled me to use plants like peonies, hydrangeas, lilies, pulmonarias and lamiums, including *Lamium orvala*, a Dead Nettle with large heads of deep-strawberry-pink flowers which I admire very much, but which is not widely known.

Several different veronicas grow around the edge of this part of the garden. There is understandable confusion in many gardeners' minds between veronicas and parahebes. Veronicas generally behave as herbaceous plants, while parahebes form semi-woody little bushes. Both make most attractive mounds or mats to edge the borders, their neat green leaves being completely buried beneath the wealth of tiny flowers in gentian-blue or white.

Potentillas do well in the sunny beds – *Potentilla* 'Miss Willmott', and *P. atrosanguinea*, which has flowers of the rich dark red you see when a fresh drop of blood oozes from a wound. A yellow

Anaphalis
triplinervis

Agapanthus
campanulatus
'Albus'

Aster
lateriflorus
'Horizontalis'

Bergenia
x 'Admiral'

Crocosmi
'Lucife

Lavandula
'Munstead Blue'

Virburnu
davidii

Geranium
sanguineum
'Lancastriense'

Strobilan
atropurpu

Veronica
'Craterlake
Blue'

Bupleur
falcatu

Bergenia
'Margery Fis

one with an orange eye and silver strawberry-like leaves is called *P. argyrophylla*. Kniphofias are planted for their interesting late-summer and autumn spikes, including a particularly attractive one, *Kniphofia snowdenii*, which produces elegant and unusual heads of widely spaced curving coral-coloured flowers from late summer right through the autumn.

THE SUN AND SHADE BEDS

The spine of one of the beds in the Reservoir Garden contains several trees, including a cherry with wonderful peeling bark which looks like polished amber – *Prunus serrula* 'Tibetica' (although unfortunately it has insignificant flowers), a white-berried mountain ash (*Sorbus hupehensis*) and *Prunus sargentii*, a huge cherry that is very fleeting both in its flowering and its autumn colour. Some say it is one of the finest of ornamental cherries and I would agree so far as spectacular blossom is concerned, but it is not perhaps for small gardens. Its large single pink flowers are very attractive so long as your garden is not plagued with bullfinches. The tree has an elegance and style that some of the smaller ornamental cherries do not have – they are simply

Part of a border in the Reservoir Garden.

dumpy masses of blossom. Behind the cherries are mixed conifers. *Chamaecyparis lawsoniana* 'Triomphe de Boskoop' with blue foliage, the tall bright green *Thuja plicata*, a Norwegian spruce, and a Monkey Puzzle tree (*Araucaria araucana*) which is still too young to be very effective.

I like to make a mixed planting of deciduous and evergreen trees and shrubs, so there is always something to look at in the garden in winter. If it is all deciduous the garden has no form in those months, and if it is entirely evergreen, the overall impression is heavy and lumpy-looking. Yellow-leaved shrubs offer a much-needed lightening effect among other darker-leaved ones, while the partial shade from trees overhead prevents leaf scorch on tender yellow-leaved forms. The golden-leaved *Philadelphus coronarius* 'Aureus' needs a bit of pruning from time to time to encourage strong young shoots carrying the brightest coloured leaves. Although several other *Philadelphus* fill the cooler areas with wonderful perfume, I do not in fact plan for scent. But because I grow such a wide variety of plants, many perfumes — whether from flowers or foliage -- do occur throughout the garden.

On the sunny side of an island bed *Onosma albo-roseum* is a plant adapted to sunny conditions, its leaves protected by a covering of bristly hairs. When not in flower the rosettes of grey

Soft pastel colours are accented by the vivid lime-green flower heads of Euphorbia martinii. *This low-growing* Euphorbia *of dense habit provides interest whether in leaf or flower, remaining evergreen all winter. Its cumulus shape is broken by the elegant sprays of blue-flowered* Veronica perfoliata, *whose round grey leaves look like* Eucalyptus *foliage. To the right are pink-flowered spires of* Diascia rigescens *contrasting with a small group of blue flax,* Linum narbonnense, *flowering for weeks in midsummer. In the distance the soft buff haze is formed by the tall flower-heads of one of my favourite grasses,* Stipa gigantea.

Background height is provided in this picture by a young Eucalyptus niphophila. *Beside it can be seen the tracery of twigs and leaves formed by* Genista aetnensis. *A solitary spire of* Verbascum pulverulentum *has seeded into the hybrid musk rose* 'Cornelia'. *The large-flowered catmint* (Nepeta gigantea) *makes a firm foreground. Shining brown scaly buds of* Centaurea macrocephala *will prolong the picture when they open masses of yellow thread-like petals, repeating the yellow of the* Verbascum *flowers.*

FRITILLARIA

F. acmopetala
Greenish bells with dark brown markings dangle from tall graceful stems. This plant tends to produce many offspring which are slow in making flowering bulbs. For well-drained soil in a sunny position. 38cm/15in. Zone 6.

F. camtschatcensis
This extraordinary fritillary likes a rich leaf-mould soil in sun or part shade. Its curious bulb looks rather like a spoonful of cooked rice squeezed into a round ball. The bulblets can be pulled apart and grown for several years before they make a flowering stem. The green glossy leaves are set in whorls around the stems. Several open pendant bells are produced in May, up to 3cm/1¼in long. They are unbelievably black, smooth outside and heavily corrugated inside, where the colour is slightly lighter – a dark chocolate-maroon. 30–38cm/12–15in. Zone 6.

F. imperialis
The Crown Imperial is one of the first bulbs to emerge in spring, producing a pungent scent in early March. The leaves are shiny and slightly twisted, spiralling around the thick stem and ending halfway up where the stem becomes purple. The stems are topped with plumes of narrow green leaves and drooping waxy orange bells. (Another form has yellow bells.) If left to settle down, these plants will make grapefruit-sized bulbs. 1.2m/4ft. Zone 5.

There are many species of these strangely attractive bulbs in cultivation. They are found in the wild in all kinds of conditions in temperate countries around the world. Comparatively few are grown in gardens since not all are reliably hardy. The best known include the great Crown Imperial Fritillary, *Fritillaria imperialis*, and our native Snakeshead Fritillary, *F. meleagris*. The first needs deep rich soil to produce fist-sized bulbs. The latter, still found wild in a few protected water-meadows in Britain today, must have heavy retentive soil.

Apart from the conspicuous *F. imperialis*, with its 1.2m/4ft tall stems bearing orange or yellow bell-shaped flowers most are small and subdued in colour. They come and go quickly in early summer, leaving behind interesting seed-heads like ghosts of these modest but endearing plants.

F. imperialis (above)

F. meleagris
Also known as the Snakeshead Fritillary. It is easily grown provided the soil does not dry out during the growing season. The stems are lightly set with narrow blue-green leaves and carry tapering chequered bells with angular 'shoulders'. Flowers in April–May. 25cm/10in. Zone 4.

F. messanensis
Has two or three chestnut-coloured bells to each stem, which create a subtle combination if planted with the bronze and red sempervivums. Flowers in April. 30cm/1ft. Zone 7.

F. pallidiflora
This is a treasure for the garden. Broad lance-shaped grey-green leaves, carried on short thick stems, become smaller towards the tip. The lovely large pale lemon flowers, several to a stem, are overlaid with green and faint tan veining. They will grow in sun but need deep enriched soil. Flowers in April to May. 30–45cm/1–1½ft. Zone 7.

F. persica
Spires of soft-purple bells with a grape-like bloom rise from clumps of leafy stems. The stems are not really strong enough to support the blooms, but it is preferable to let them lean against another plant rather than to tie them. Plant in a warm well-drained site under a wall. 60cm/2ft. Zone 6.

F. pontica
The leaves are fat and glaucous and the bells too

are fat, in shaded green with pale chestnut markings, carried one or two to a stem. 30cm/1ft. Zone 7.

F. pyrenaica
Each stem carries two or three matt chocolate-coloured bells in April, their bottom edges slightly curled to reveal a shiny yellow-green lining. 15–30cm/6–12in. Zone 7.

F. tuntasia
Narrow twisted grey leaves spiral around short stems. The small open bells are dark purple, almost black, overlaid with a silvery

bloom. Ideal for raised beds. 30cm/1ft. Zone 7.

F. verticillata
Slender stems rise from a bulb set with whorls of narrow blue-green leaves, thinner towards the top of the stem where their tips become tendrils. The April flowers are open and bell-shaped, pale green with brown chequering inside. Each bulb produces several offsets. It has a reputation for shy flowering but once established on warm, well-drained, well-fed soil, will flower freely. 45cm/1½ft. Zone 7.

F. tuntasia

F. meleagris

F. messanensis

F. verticillata

For years we incorrectly called this tall candelabra-type mullein Verbascum olympicum. *We now rather cautiously call it* V. pulverulentum. *The beautiful leaves, heavily coated with white felt, suggest we might be right. Often standing 1.8–2.4m/6–8ft tall, several flower-spikes make fine verticals in a large border, especially while background trees develop. For smaller spaces,* V. chaixii *stands 60–120cm/2–4ft tall, depending on the richness of growing conditions. Its densely cut spires of flowers, either white or yellow, have attractive mauve eyes.*

leaves make an interesting feature or foil for another plant in flower alongside. The flowers appear in spring from the centre of each rosette. Tightly rolled clusters or croziers of coral-pink buds open white tubular flowers. It can look even better when allowed to droop like a shawl over the edge of a low wall or rock face.

One of the smaller shrubs worth singling out for special mention is *Salix helvetica*. Most of us before we learn differently think of willows only as weeping willows, or the tall Silver Willow, both needing damp soil, but there are quite a number of others which make attractive compact bushes for ordinary garden soil. *S. helvetica* has a very distinctive character. It forms a compact round shape (not unlike a gooseberry bush) about 90cm/3ft high and across, with every part – twigs, leaves and catkins – dusted with pearly grey. While still leafless in early spring, yellow catkins explode from conspicuous amber buds. Throughout summer grey-green leaves, backed with white, make a good background for other plants.

Beneath the willow, *Haplopappus coronopifolius* makes cushions of finely cut evergreen foliage which continue to produce a succession of bright orange daisy flowers from midsummer until December. The bright green leaves make good contrast with the grey-leaved helianthemums nearby. Too much unalleviated grey foliage can look very flat and uninteresting. Helianthemums come in many varieties, with green, grey or variegated leaves, with single or double flowers in many shades from white to crimson and cream to orange. They are liable to be damaged by very cold winters, but even in cold gardens or heavy soils, this problem can be lessened if attention is paid to the drainage.

Walking round the Reservoir Garden in winter, the eye is caught by long-lasting designs created with foliage alone. *Libertia ixioides*, with its dense tufts of narrow leaves stained orange, harmonizes pleasantly with spreading carpets of golden-leaved thymes. But I do not always place plants the first time in a way that pleases me, even though I am planting all the time. For example, I have some pinks in this bed – the old-fashioned clove-scented buttonhole carnations, including a red one and pink-and-white striped one. When I planted them here I needed a home for them, but they look out of context, I think, and the flowers, though lovely to pick, do not mix with the species flowers of the rest of the planting. I shall probably move them to a picking border.

The views opposite are part of a large area of well-drained soil devoted primarily to bulbous plants.
As the waves of Narcissus (below left) and deep blue Scilla sibirica *recede, their leaves are partially buried in fast-growing, fragile-looking* Corydalis ochroleuca, *the white-flowered form of yellow fumitory. Also rushing up fast are the tall lily-like Crown Imperials (Fritillaria imperialis), hastening to open lemon-yellow or burnt-orange bells (below right). The strong fox-like scent of their foliage makes the heart beat at this early evocation of spring when the days are still cold. Throughout April many other fritillaries appear, including the green-flowered F. verticillata, chocolate-brown F. pyrenaica and the soft chestnut bells of F. messanensis. All need warm, well-drained soil. Fritillaria meleagris, our native Snakeshead Fritillary, is planted in areas of damper, heavier soil.*

THE BULB BED

Putting bulbs in only one area of the garden solves the problem of their over-abundant leaves. They look charming as bright clusters of flowers, but these are followed by copious bundles of long leaves which lie about on the more choice cover plants leaving them with dead and dreary patches by the time the bulb leaves have faded and can be removed. In other parts of the garden I do plant bulbs that lose their leaves very early on, like erythroniums, or those that have good-mannered leaves like *Fritillaria meleagris*. I am experimenting with an area devoted predominantly to bulbs, with here and there a few tough perennial herbaceous plants to prolong the flowering season.

The year begins with drifts of a fine snowdrop, *Galanthus caucasicus*, quickly followed by small-flowered daffodils, including the species *Narcissus minor, N. pallida* and the hybrid, 'W. P. Millner'. Providing lush foliage in the early spring are the shining leaf clusters of *Colchicum speciosum* (which produces purple goblet-shaped flowers in autumn) and clumps of *Iris foetidissima*. These are followed by a range of fritillaries, some of which are shown on pages 156–7.

I use smaller herbaceous plants to edge the bed, including *Geranium tuberosum*, an early-summer flowering plant with an airy mass of tiny pink-and-white flowers standing about 30cm/12in high. *Corydalis solida*, with mauve-blue flowers, and *C. bulbosa* 'Alba', with taller spires of creamy-white flowers, appear between blue scillas or purple erythroniums – they all vanish completely by mid-May until the following spring. There are groups of *Anemone blanda* 'Bridesmaid' whose pure white flowers stand out like patches of unmelted snow in the cold bareness of early spring.

THE SCOPE FOR REPLANTING

The planting here still has a long way to go; it is a bit like a teenager, this part of the garden, with plenty of future promise but not yet quite mature. At the moment I feel it is a little lacking in character.

However, every gardener has to learn a lot from trial and error. Books can be helpful but you cannot completely copy the way someone else has planted their garden, although you can learn gradually by reading, by studying other people's gardens and conditions, and by experimenting yourself.

As a beginner it helps to keep a few simple rules in mind. Think of the overall outline you wish eventually to achieve and then make a list of plants to provide height, bulk and cover. Start with a small range of plants and be prepared to alter the bed as the planting matures. Later, with more knowledge and experience, new species can be introduced to extend the range and interest of the planting.

Top left: this early autumn scene shows an area relying almost on foliage alone, after the summer glory of Philadelphus *and lace-cap hydrangeas have faded. Stealing the scene is a flowering patch of* Pulmonaria saccharata, *its boldly spotted leaf rosettes at their best throughout late summer and autumn. The running fern,* Dennstaedtia punctiloba, *is bright green all summer, becoming honey-gold before it disappears underground for winter.*

Left: sheaves of tall narrow leaves and brown seed-heads of Crocosmia 'Lucifer' *have been tumbled by autumn winds and rain, but beneath them comfortable clumps of an evergreen* Bergenia *hybrid give a feeling of solidity to the border edge. Stiffly bushy plants of* Aster lateriflorus 'Horizontalis' *carry thousands of tiny starry mauve-pink flowers while the green seed-heads and yellowing foliage of the hardy* Agapanthus campanulatus *highlight the border.*

Left: the sadly leaning tree in this picture was a result of the hurricane of October '87 when many trees in the garden were damaged or uprooted. But when we had finished mourning the losses, it became apparent that new areas for planting had been opened up which would rejuvenate the garden. Making the decision to cull trees is always painful, but should not be left until it is too late.

Plant Guide

The following is a cultivation guide for some of the perennials I use. Large groups of particularly useful foliage plants have been singled out earlier in the book and are simply cross-referenced here. There are many more perennials that could have been included (and that I sell through my nursery), but in the space available I have tried to provide a mixture of the more familiar and useful perennials together with some exciting and unusual ones.

The plant hardiness zone at the end of each entry relates to the zones in common use in North America. They are a general guide to the annual average minimum temperatures that the plant in question will withstand. Hardiness ratings are far from an exact science, as many factors play a part in the plant's ability to withstand cold, including the chill factor of the wind, whether the plant was turgid when the first frosts arrived and whether the soil is free-draining or not. It serves, however, as a rough general guide to the plants that will grow in a particular area and it would be unwise to try to grow any plant that is obviously outside the temperature range for your area.

Plant Hardiness Zones

Zone	C°	F°
1	below −46°	below −50°
2	−46° to −40°	−50° to −40°
3	−40° to −34°	−40° to −30°
4	−34° to −28°	−30° to −20°
5	−28° to −22°	−20° to −10°
6	−22° to −16°	−10° to 0°
7	−16° to −12°	0° to 10°
8	−12° to −6°	10° to 20°
9	−6° to −1°	20° to 30°
10	−1° to 4°	30° to 40°

ACANTHUS

A. mollis This imposing plant has large, deeply cut, glossy green leaves which make a feature all the year round unless winters are exceptionally hard. Tall flower stems carry curiously hooded purple and white flowers in late summer. It needs sun and good drainage.
Up to 1.5m/5ft. ZONE 7.

ACHILLEA

A. decolorans 'W. B. Child' Slender stems bear white flowers arranged in a loose flat head. Main flowering in June, but often again in late autumn. This needs sun and retentive soil.
60cm/2ft. ZONE 3.
A. filipendulina (*eupatorium*) **'Gold Plate'** Well known with its tall, stiff stems bearing flat heads of tiny yellow flowers. Dries excellently, retaining its colour. Flowers midsummer. For full sun and needs good drainage.
90cm/3ft. ZONE 3.
A. 'Moonshine' Valued for its flat heads of pale clear yellow, held on branching stems above beautiful silvery grey foliage. Good to cut and dries well retaining colour.

Flowers in midsummer and again often in autumn. It needs well-drained soil in sun.
60cm/2ft. ZONE 6.

ACORUS

A. calamus 'Variegatus' Handsome sword-like leaves boldly variegated cream and green with rose-pink bases in spring. Deliciously spicy scent when crushed in the hand. Flowers of no merit. Needs damp soil, or shallow water.
90cm/3ft. ZONE 3.

AGAPANTHUS

The following forms are both hardy in well-drained but well-fed soil and sun. All flower throughout August, pick well and make good green or dried seed-heads in September. In very cold situations a winter mulch is necessary for protection.
A. campanulatus 'Albus' From clumps of strap-shaped leaves appear smooth bare stems carrying round heads of close-set, white, trumpet-shaped flowers.
60cm/2ft. ZONE 7.
A. campanulatus 'Cobalt Blue' An extra fine blue.
60cm/2ft. ZONE 7.

AJUGA

All the ajugas like sun or part-shade and retentive soil.
A. reptans One of our native woodland carpeting plants. There are several good coloured-leaf forms to be found, including one with deep purple, highly polished leaves called **A.r. 'Atropurpurea'** with spikes of deep blue flowers.
25cm/10in. ZONE 3.
A. reptans 'Alba' Makes quickly spreading carpets of green, bronze-tinted crinkly leaves held in rosettes. Attractive spires of white-lipped flowers in May.
10cm/4in. ZONE 4.
A. reptans 'Burgundy Glow' Beautiful foliage suffused rose and

Ajuga reptans 'Atropurpurea'

magenta, regularly edged with cream. Vivid carpet all winter. Flowers blue.
10cm/4in. ZONE 4.

ALCHEMILLA

Alchemillas thrive in sun or part-shade and retentive soil.

A. conjuncta For those who look closely, a charming plant. Small exquisitely cut leaves are backed with shining silk which forms a silver edge on the top side. Tiny green flowers held in small bobbles turn red as they age.
10cm/4in. ZONE 3.

A. mollis Invaluable in the garden and for picking. Forms a mound of velvety rounded leaves. When their serrated edges are full of dew-drops each leaf looks like a beaded shawl. For weeks in midsummer the long sprays of frothing lime-green starry flowers are a delight.
45cm/1½ft. ZONE 3.

ALLIUM

(See page 148.)

ANAPHALIS

A. triplinervis 'Summer Snow' Makes slowly spreading clumps of felt-grey foliage topped with clusters of pearly-white everlasting daisies in late summer. Hang them to dry for winter flower arranging. Plant in sun in retentive soil.
25cm/10in. ZONE 3.

ANEMONE

A. fulgens Flowers in spring with *Euphorbia polychroma* and *E. wulfenii*, making a startling contrast of intense, black-eyed, scarlet blooms, against the green-tinged gold of the spurges. It needs well-drained soil and sun.
23cm/9in. ZONE 6.

A. magellanica Neat clumps of dark green, finely cut leaves are a

setting for cool lemon-yellow flowers in spring, followed by large, woolly seed-heads. This also needs sun and good drainage.
30–38cm/12–15in. ZONE 5.

A. nemorosa 'Allenii' A lovely blue form of the wild Wood Anemone. In spring, nodding buds, stained purplish-rose, open to the sun breath-taking flowers filled with yellow stamens. Best in retentive leaf-mould soil, in part shade.
10cm/4in. ZONES 4–5.

ANGELICA

A. archangelica A great plant valued for both its architectural effect and its delicate flavour. In its second year there rises from the broad divided leaves a stout branching stem ending in wide heads of Cow Parsley-like flowers in late summer. The green seed-heads are most decorative. The young hollow stems can be preserved in sugar. Unfortunately, it is biennial, but it is well worth while carefully placing a few seedlings for the following year. Grows in damp retentive soil in sun or part shade.
2–2½m/6–8ft. ZONE 6.

ANTHEMIS

All forms of *A. tinctoria* need to be replanted occasionally in refreshed and retentive soil to retain vigorous, free-flowering clumps, and all need full sun.

A. tinctoria 'E. C. Buxton' Above a low neat mound of ferny green leaves, thin stiff stems carry creamy-yellow daisies endlessly throughout the summer.
50cm/20in. ZONE 3.

A. tinctoria 'Wargrave Variety' Much admired for its cool lemon-yellow flowers; looks well with *Euphorbia griffithii* 'Fireglow'.
75cm/2½ft. ZONE 3.

ARTEMISIA

With their beautiful silver, highly aromatic foliage these plants are invaluable as ground cover or background plants in the hot, dry garden where there is plenty of sun and good drainage. In all artemisias the foliage is valued more than the flowers, which are insignificant.

A. abrotanum Also known as Southernwood or Lad's Love. Plant this deliciously aromatic plant beside a path or sitting area. It makes a shrubby plant densely set with whorls of feathery, sage-green foliage, lovely contrast for salvias or cistuses. Spring pruning keeps it well shaped.
75cm/2½ft. ZONES 3–4.

A. dracunculus The true French Tarragon. Narrow green foliage adds very distinctive flavour to salads, chicken and fish dishes.
60cm/2ft. ZONES 6–7.

A. pontica Forms a miniature forest of stiff, upright stems clothed in finely cut silver-grey scented foliage. Excellent feature and ground cover in dry sunny places. Spreads by underground stems.
45cm/1½ft. ZONES 7–8.

ARUM

A. italicum 'Pictum' (of gardens) These exotic leaves unroll from the leafmould in late autumn, continuing to grow throughout the winter, bowing beneath bitter frost, but standing undamaged immediately it thaws. By April they are the full height, dark-glossy green, spear-shaped and veined with ivory. In September appear stems of red berries.
38cm/15in. ZONE 6.

ARUNCUS

Aruncus are best in sun or half shade and retentive soil.

A. aethusifolius Produces low clumps of fresh green leaves as

Evergreen plants
(Warm well-drained soil)
Achillea filipendulina
A. 'Moonshine'
Anthemis tinctoria
Artemisia (most)
Ballota
Cistus
Dianthus
Eryngium agavifolium
Euphorbia polychroma
E. wulfenii
Grindelia
Lavandula
Leucanthemum
Libertia
Ruta
Salvia officinalis
Santolina
Sedum spurium
Thymus

(Retentive soil in sun)
Ajuga
Bergenia
Geranium (some)
Helleborus
Heuchera
× *Heucherella*
Ophiopogon
Penstemon (partly)
Phlomis russeliana
Potentilla tabernaemontani
Viola

(In cool conditions)
Arum italicum 'Pictum'
Chrysanthemum parthenium
Epimedium
Euphorbia robbiae
Hedera
Helleborus
Heuchera
× *Heucherella*
Mitella
Ophiopogon
Pachysandra
Phlox stolonifera
Pulmonaria
Saxifraga
Symphytum grandiflorum
Tellima
Tiarella
Vinca
Viola
Waldsteinia

Aruncus dioicus

finely cut as chervil but with more substance. A forest of wiry flower stems rises 30–35cm/12–14in high, carrying tiny astilbe-like heads of small creamy-white flowers in June. By September they are still attractive, with barren heads tinted light chestnut, while seed-bearing heads are dark shining brown and foliage develops pink and reddish autumn tints.
25–30cm/10–12in. ZONE 3.
A. dioicus (*sylvester*) Also known as Goat's Beard. A superb plant. Forms large clumps of elegant light-green foliage above which rise great creamy plumes of tiny flowers in midsummer. Interesting seed-heads. Needs rich soil.
120cm/4ft. ZONE 3.

ASPHODELINE

Both these plants are for sunny areas with good drainage.
A. liburnica Comes into flower when *A. lutea* is already forming seed-heads. Similar but much more delicately made; branched heads of much paler yellow flowers – effective in late summer.
90cm/3ft. ZONE 7.

A. lutea Tall stems bear whorls of grey-blue grassy leaves. Strap-petalled, star-like flowers of bright yellow. The seed-pods form a wand of bright green cherries which eventually turn brown.
90cm/3ft. ZONE 6.

ASPHODELUS

A. albus Seen everywhere around the Mediterranean on dry, stony soils, it thrives in sunny areas with good drainage. From fleshy roots it produces a huddle of long narrow leaves above which stand tall, smooth, strong branching stems topped with spires of long narrow buds which open in early summer to starry-white flowers, warmed by a soft brown vein running down the centre of each petal.
120cm/4ft. ZONE 7.

ASTER

All prefer retentive soil, in sun.
A. amellus 'Violet Queen' An excellent old variety. Stiff dark stems carry open heads of intense violet well-shaped flowers throughout September and October.
38cm/15in. ZONE 4.

A. divaricatus (*corymbosus*) Gertrude Jekyll showed us how to plant this among bergenias where its thin shiny black stems, topped with frothy sprays of tiny, white, pink-flushed daisies, are supported.
60cm/2ft ZONE 4.
A. ericoides 'Esther' Makes a low loose bouquet of small lilac-rose flowers in autumn.
38cm/15in. ZONE 4.
A. × *frikartii* 'Mönch' Without doubt the best Michaelmas Daisy. Large bold flowers, rich lavender-blue. Flowers from August until October.
75cm/2½ft. ZONE 4.

Aster ericoides 'Esther'

A. thompsonii 'Nanus' Valued for its charming habit of growth and very long flowering season from August until the end of October. Neat clumps of narrow petalled tiny-eyed clear-blue flowers.
45cm/18in. ZONE 4.

ASTILBE

A. chinensis 'Pumila' Slowly spreads into a weed-smothering carpet of broadly cut foliage. Slender spikes of rosy-mauve flowers from late summer to autumn. Like all the astilbes, it needs sun and moist soil.
30cm/1ft. ZONE 4.

Drought-loving plants
(Small and low-growing)
Allium (dwarf forms)
Anemone fulgens
Calamintha
Crepis incana
Dianthus
Diascia
Eriophyllum
Gypsophila (dwarf forms)
Haplopappus
Leucanthemum
Linum salsoloides
Melissa
Sedum (dwarf forms)
Sempervivum
Sideritis
Thymus
Zauschneria

A. simplicifolia 'Bronze Elegance'
A beautiful dwarf hybrid. Green foliage darkened with bronze shadows makes a perfect base for arching sprays of tiny flowers which combine cream and salmon-pink. July to August.
30cm/1ft. ZONE 4.

A. taquetii 'Superba' This unusual *Astilbe* flowers in late summer when most of the other astilbes are over. Tall stately stems carry large dense spires of fluffy rosy-mauve flowers which look well near *Rudbeckia fulgida* or the lovely pale lemon *Lysimachia ciliata*. It is an easy strong plant and will stand full sun if it has retentive soil.
120cm/4ft. ZONE 4.

ASTRANTIA

A. major 'Sunningdale Variety'
Possibly the most beautiful variegated foliage plant in spring. The large hand-shaped and pointed leaves are elegantly marked with yellow and cream. Branching stems of white pink-flushed posy flowers are an added summer and autumn bonus.
75cm/2½. ZONE 5.

BALLOTA

B. pseudodictamnus One of the loveliest greys. From a woody base spring long curving stems of round leaves clothed in grey-white felt. Tiny mauve flowers are buried in felty green bobbles held along the length of curving stems, very desirable to cut. The drier the conditions the whiter the foliage becomes, so good drainage is important. Grows best in full sun.
75cm/2½ft. ZONE 8.

BAPTISIA

B. australis A superior lupin-like plant needing sun and deep retentive soil. Slim spires of rich blue flowers in summer followed by clusters of black swollen seed-pods on dark, stiffly upright stems.
90cm/3ft. ZONE 3.

BERGENIA
(See page 38.)

BRUNNERA

B. macrophylla In spring, long sprays of tiny forget-me-not-blue flowers are followed by robust clumps of basal leaves, each huge and heart-shaped, making good ground cover in shade or part shade and retentive soil.
45cm/1½ft. ZONE 3.

B. macrophylla 'Hadspen Cream'
Large light-green leaves are bordered with primrose.
45cm/1½ft. ZONE 3.

BUTOMUS

B. umbellatus Grows in shallow water in bogs. Sheaves of stiff grassy leaves make fine verticals. Flower-stems carry umbels of rose-pink flowers in midsummer.
120cm/4ft. ZONE 6.

CALAMINTHA

C. grandiflora Useful for the edge of a well-drained, sunny border, neat little bushes of fresh green foliage, dotted with rose-pink blossoms all summer.
25cm/10in. ZONE 6.

C. nepetoides Charming in late summer with clouds of tiny pale-blue flowers on bushy aromatic plants. Loved by bees.
30cm/1ft. ZONE 7.

CALTHA

C. palustris 'Alba' The lovely white form of the Marsh Marigold. From early spring to midsummer. It grows in wet, boggy areas.
15cm/6in. ZONE 3.

C. palustris 'Plena' The double Marsh Marigold, whose golden flowers come as early as the single form but last longer. Spring.
30cm/1ft. ZONE 3.

CAMASSIA

These are bulbous plants from the rich meadows of North-west

Drought-loving plants
(Medium to large)
Acanthus
Achillea filipendulina
A. 'Moonshine'
Agapanthus
Allium
Anthemis tinctoria
Asphodeline
Asphodelus
Ballota
Cirsium rivulare
  atropurpureum
Cistus
Crambe
Crinum
Crocosmia
Cynara
Eryngium
Euphorbia polychroma
E. wulfenii
Foeniculum
Gaura
Gladiolus papilio
Glaucium
Grindelia
Lavandula
Linaria
Linum flavum
Onopordum
Penstemon
Perovskia
Phlomis
Ruta graveolens
Salvia
Santolina
Sedum 'Autumn Joy'
S. spectabile
Senecio
Stachys
Verbascum

**Camassia quamash
'Electra'**

Ground-covering plants

Achillea
Ajuga
Alchemilla
Anaphalis
Anthemis
Ballota
Bergenia
Brunnera
Campanula carpatica
  turbinata
Crambe cordifolia
Dianthus
Diascia
Dicentra
Epilobium glabellum
Epimedium
Erigeron
Eriophyllum
Euphorbia
Geranium
Geum
Hedera
Helleborus
Heuchera
Hosta
Lamium
Lysimachia
Melissa
Myosotis
Omphalodes
Pachyphragma
Pachysandra
Peltiphyllum
Petasites
Phlomis
Phlox stolonifera
Polygonum bistorta
  'Superbum'
Pulmonaria
Rubus tricolor
Salvia officinalis
Santolina
Saxifraga caucasica
S. × urbium
Sedum
Senecio
Stachys
Symphytum
Tellima
Thymus
Tiarella
Trachystemon
Trifolium
Verbena corymbosa
Vinca
Viola
Waldsteinia
Zauschneria

America, valued vertical features in early summer, either in borders or naturalized. They need retentive soil and sun.
C. cusickii Strong flower-stems carry spires of ice-blue narrow-petalled star-shaped flowers in May.
90–120cm/3–4ft. ZONE 5.
C. esculenta Has shorter stems of dark-blue flowers, also in May.
30cm/1ft. ZONE 5.
C. quamash 'Electra' Extra large heads of lavender-blue flowers.
90cm/3ft. ZONE 6.

CAMPANULA

C. burghaltii Deep purple-blue buds contrast with the large palest-blue open bells which dangle from slender stems. An irresistible plant. Early summer, and again in autumn. Best in sun and retentive soil.
45cm/1½ft. ZONE 6.
C. carpatica turbinata (of gardens) A gem among dwarf campanulas. Free-flowering, tidy clumps smothered beneath rich-blue saucer-shaped flowers. Mid- to late summer.
30cm/1ft. ZONE 3.
C. lactiflora A splendid sight when stout, leafy stems are crowned with great heads of powder-blue bell flowers. Well placed among shrubs, especially shrub roses. Mid- and late summer.
1.5m/5ft. ZONE 7.

CENTAUREA

C. pulchra 'Major' (of gardens) A most handsome plant. From a base of strong silver-grey cut leaves rise stiff stems bearing large knobbly buds of overlapping transparent silver scales which open into striking cyclamen-pink flowers. Midsummer. It requires sun and good drainage.
90cm/3ft. ZONE 7.

CHAEROPHYLLUM

C. hirsutum 'Roseum' This lovely Cow Parsley is one of the joys of early summer. Over a base of feathery leaves stand branching stems, each holding a flat-topped head of tiny lilac-mauve flowers. Likes sun or part shade in good, retentive soil.
60cm/2ft. ZONE 3.

CHRYSANTHEMUM

C. 'Emperor of China' This old hybrid has beautifully quilled petals, deep crimson in the centre but fading to silver-pink as the layers of petals unroll. By flowering time (November), the foliage becomes suffused and veined with rich crimson. Best in sun and retentive soil.
90–120cm/3–4ft. ZONE 5.
C. parthenium 'Aureum' Lime-yellow, finely divided foliage throughout the year. Sprays of tiny white daisies throughout summer. Grows in sun or part shade in retentive soil.
30cm/1ft. ZONE 4.

C. rubellum 'Clara Curtis' One of the best late-summer-flowering plants, forming domes of blossom composed of single clear-pink daisy flowers. Divide it in spring every few years and plant in full sun, in fertile, well-drained retentive soil.
75cm/2½ft. ZONE 4.
C. uliginosum A beautiful fresh feature for the end of the season, in grass, among shrubs, or in a big border. Strong clumps of stiff leafy stems carry sprays of green-eyed chalk-white daisies. They turn to face the sun, throughout October. Good to pick.
2m/6ft. ZONE 3.

CIMICIFUGA

C. simplex 'Elstead' Differs from 'White Pearl' in having purplish stems and buds which open creamy-white with pink stamens. For shady areas and retentive soil.
120cm/4ft. ZONE 3.
C. simplex 'White Pearl' For a cool shady place, not dry. A most elegant plant in autumn. Branching stems carry snowy-white

Chrysanthemum parthenium 'Aureum' with *Pachysandra terminalis*

166

bottle-brushes 10–13cm/4–5in long. These develop into a most desirable lime-green seed-head. 120cm/4ft. ZONE 3.

CISTUS

All cistuses flower from July to August and require well-drained soil and sun.

C. × corbariensis Forms a medium-sized bush of light-green crinkled foliage. Flower-buds pink, opening to white cups. 120cm/4ft. ZONE 8.

C. cyprius The dark-green, slightly sticky foliage makes an excellent background all the year in the dry garden, but in midsummer, covered with huge white flowers splotched with purple, it commands admiration. 150cm/5ft. ZONE 8.

C. × purpureus Fresh green foliage all year, slightly crinkled, smothered in summer with large rich-pink flowers, each with a purple splash. 120cm/4ft. ZONE 8.

COLCHICUM

C. speciosum 'Album' In retentive soil and sun, this produces superb white flowers, rounded, like large wine goblets on pale-green stems, to be treasured. 15cm/6in. ZONE 6.

C. speciosum 'Atrorubens' A rare wine-purple form with purple-stained stems. Plant in full sun. 15cm/6in. ZONE 6.

CORYDALIS

C. bulbosa Flowers a little later with taller spires of cream or deep purple flowers. Retentive soil in part-shade. 15–20cm/6–8in. ZONE 5.

C. cheilanthifolia Attracts admiration with its soft mounds of finely dissected fern-like leaves.

Corydalis bulbosa

They are soft olive-green, a perfect complement to the long succession of light yellow flowers in early summer. 25–30cm/10–12in. ZONE 4.

C. solida A fleeting delight in early spring. From bulbous roots this corydalis produces finely cut blue-grey leaves which are just right for the delicate heads of plum-purple flowers. Retentive soil in part-shade. 8–10cm/3–4in. ZONE 5.

CRAMBE

C. cordifolia From a mound of huge green leaves, bare branching stems soar skywards, carrying wide clouds of starry white flowers in July, like a giant *Gypsophila*. Needs sun and retentive soil. 2m/6ft. ZONE 7.

CREPIS

C. incana This unusual dandelion is enchanting in late summer. Over tight rosettes of grey-green deeply cut leaves stand sprays of many-petalled soft rose-pink flowers. Plant in well-drained soil in sun. 23–30cm/9–12in. ZONE 7.

CRINUM

C. × powellii A bulbous plant. From the top of stout purplish stems tumble large trumpet-like rose-pink flowers for several weeks in late summer. Usually grown against a warm wall, flourishes in sun and retentive soil in open ground, if well drained, well fed and well mulched in winter. Good in tubs. 120cm/4ft. ZONE 8.

C. × powellii 'Album' Large beautifully shaped pure-white trumpets. Both these crinums are deliciously scented. 120cm/4ft. ZONE 8.

CROCOSMIA

C. 'Citronella' Soft creamy-yellow flowers, abundantly produced in late summer. It needs sun and good drainage. 60cm/2ft. ZONE 7.

C. 'Lucifer' This imposing plant has stiff pleated blade-shaped leaves topped with large heads of brilliant flame-red flowers, from June to July. 120cm/4ft. ZONE 7.

CYCLAMEN

C. coum A group of varying forms, some with green leaves, others with silver marbling on green. The leaves can be round or kidney shaped. From spring onwards the flowers in shades from white to rich carmine are produced. 5cm/2in. ZONE 4.

C. hederifolium (*neapolitanum*) Also known as the Ivy-Leafed Cyclamen. Attractive large leaves

Plants for waterside and bog
Astilbe
Caltha
Euphorbia palustris
Gunnera
Hemerocallis
Houttuynia
Inula
Iris kaempferi
I. pseudacorus
Ligularia
Lysichitum
Lysimachia
Lythrum
Myosotis
Peltiphyllum
Petasites
Polygonum bistorta
Pontederia
Ranunculus acris 'Flore Pleno'
R. speciosus plenus
Rodgersia
Senecio smithii
Trollius
Verbena corymbosa
Zantedeschia

Cyclamen hederifolium 'Album'

patterned with silver and flowers in shades from white (*C.h.* 'Alba') to pink. Increases freely if left undisturbed.
10cm/4in. ZONE 4.

DENTARIA

D. digitata (*Cardamine pentaphyllos*) A spring delight for cool retentive soil in shade. Fine cut leaves and nodding flower-stems unroll together, the flowers soft lilac, like large cuckoo flowers.
30–38cm/12–15in. ZONE 6.

Digitalis lutea × *D. purpurea*

DIANTHUS

The following pinks are all valued as good cover-plants in sun and dry well-drained soil, making tidy close plants. There are many more available. Most flower in midsummer.
D. deltoides The Maiden Pink. Abundant little starry flowers of carmine stand for weeks over solid mats of dark green foliage. Lovely with thymes.
20cm/8in. ZONE 3.
***D.* 'Mrs Sinkins'** The heavily scented old favourite pink, used for edging cottage garden paths, has fully double blooms of creamy-white. Midsummer.
23cm/9in. ZONE 5.
***D.* 'Sops in Wine'** The single wine-red flowers have a white patch on each petal.
15cm/6in. ZONE 5.

DIASCIA

D. cordata **'Ruby Field'** This good form floats sprays of salmon-pink nemesia-like flowers over neat flat mats of small green leaves. Enchanting, mid- to late summer.
15cm/6in. ZONE 7.
D. rigescens This plant produces taller, stiffer stems of rose-pink flowers than *D. cordata*, in flower from June until October. Said to be

Digitalis purpurea 'Alba'

hardy, but overwintering cuttings under shelter would be a worth-while precaution. Both need sun and good drainage.
30–38cm/12–15in. ZONE 7.

DICENTRA

D. spectabilis Also known as Bleeding Heart, or Lady's Locket. Needs rich, deep retentive soil in shade or part shade to produce tall stems drooping with the delicate rose and white lockets. Flowers early summer.
60cm/2ft. ZONE 5.
D. spectabilis **'Alba'** Above delicately cut green leaves arch green stems bowed with beautiful ivory-white, heart-shaped lockets. Flowers for weeks in late spring and early summer.
75cm/2½ft. ZONE 5.

DIGITALIS

D. ferruginea A gem. This perennial Foxglove sends up tall flower-stems bearing in midsummer close-set rounded buds which open to smallish short trumpets of coppery-yellow,

Digitalis parviflora

veined brown. Grows in sun or part shade provided it has good drainage.
90cm/3ft. ZONE 5.
D. lutea Sends up tall spikes of small, slim, pale yellow flowers.
120cm/4ft. ZONE 4.
D. parviflora Small copper-coloured flowers on a short stout flower stem.
60cm/2ft. ZONE 5.
D. purpurea **'Alba'** A white-flowered form of the native Foxglove. Best in part shade.
120cm/4ft plus. ZONE 3.

DISPORUM

D. sessile **'Variegatum'** From a wandering starfish-shaped rootstock rise slender stems bearing pretty fresh green leaves, broadly striped with cream. Creamy-white bell-shaped flowers dangle beneath the leaves in spring. It likes part shade and retentive soil.
30–38cm/12–15in. ZONE 4.

ECHINACEA

E. purpurea An imposing plant with fine dark foliage carried on stiff branching stems that need no staking. Large broad-petalled flowers of rich mauve-crimson are enhanced by central cones which glisten orange-brown. Long flower-ing period from late summer. Plant in sun in retentive soil.
90cm/3ft. ZONE 3.

EPILOBIUM

E. angustifolium **'Album'** Also known as Rose Bay Willow Herb. Tall stems carry slender spires of pure-white flowers, enhanced by star-shaped green sepals. Spires of unopened buds above open flowers, with rows of pale sterile seed-pods below, maintain interesting form and colour for weeks, in late summer. Slowly

invasive. Does best in retentive soil and sun.
1–1.5m/3–5ft. ZONE 7.
E. glabellum Another Willow Herb but much smaller. Valuable ground cover; showers of creamy-white funnels from June to October
23cm/9in. ZONE 7.

EPIMEDIUM

Most valued and beautiful foliage plants which will put up with dry shade or part shade but make superb ground cover more quickly in rich damp retentive leaf-mould. Best cut down in early March to reveal the delicate sprays of tiny columbine-like flowers.
E. grandiflorum (*macranthum*) Small new leaves in spring are beige-brown, above which are held sprays of mauve-pink flowers. As they mature the leaves turn light green. Sun or part shade.
23cm/9in. ZONE 4.
E. grandiflorum 'White Queen' Exquisite large long-spurred flowers of gauzy whiteness, faintly stained with purple.
25cm/10in. ZONE 4.
E. × rubrum A splendid ground cover in shade and among shrubs. Elegant heart-shaped leaves on wiry stems emerge in soft tints of bronze-red, fading to light green, but assume vivid coral-red shades in autumn. Rose-pink flowers in spring.
23cm/9in. ZONE 4.
E. × youngianum 'Niveum' Neat clumps of smaller foliage in soft shades of milk-chocolate in spring, over which float clouds of pure white starry flowers. A gem.
25cm/10in. ZONE 5.

EREMURUS

Also called Foxtail Lily – a spectacular perennial plant. They produce straight unbranched stems, crowded along their upper

Eremurus robustus

parts with small star-shaped lily flowers. There are several species and hybrids, differing only in size and shades of white, pink and yellow. Perhaps the most spectacular is *E. robustus*.
2.5m/8ft. ZONE 5.

ERIGERON

Ideal edge-of-border plants. They look lovely with ajugas and flower continuously till frosts. They need sun and retentive soil.
E. 'Dimity' Makes tidy clumps of evergreen leaves with succession of pinkish-mauve daisies in mid-summer.
30cm/1ft. ZONE 7.

ERIOGONUM

E. umbellatum Exciting and unusual for the border edge or rock garden. Thin woody stems underpin a sprawling mat of tough grey-green leaves held in open rosettes on wire-thin reddish stalks. From the centre of each appear umbels of yellow-green buds, opening acid lemon-yellow flowers in early summer. Needs well-drained soil and sun.
15cm/6in. ZONE 7.

ERIOPHYLLUM

E. lanatum Very useful ground

cover in sun-parched but well-drained soil – quickly makes large patches of silvery-white finely divided leaves, with a show of orange-yellow daisies from late spring to early summer.
15cm/6in. ZONE 7.

ERYTHRONIUM

All erythroniums do best in rich leafy retentive soil, in part shade.
E. dens-canis The matt, chocolate-blotched, oval leaves of the Dog's Tooth Violet are as attractive as the delicate rosy-mauve flowers whose petals reflex like cyclamens in spring sunshine. Forms bundles of ivory-white pointed corms in leaf-mould soil.
15cm/6in. ZONE 6.
E. 'White Beauty' Pale cream lily-shaped flowers reflex to show cream stamens with a ring of reddish stain at their base. Broad wavy shining leaves, slightly marbled.
25cm/10in. ZONE 6.

EUPHORBIA
(See page 140.)

FOENICULUM

F. vulgare purpureum The Bronze Fennel forms clumps of tall lush green stems covered with a cloud of bronzy-brown foliage. Yellow Cow Parsley-like flowers in late summer. Handsome throughout summer and autumn. Plant in well-drained sunny areas.
1.5m/5ft. ZONE 7.

FRITILLARIA
(See page 156.)

GALANTHUS

In the wild there are a surprising number of different species of snowdrop. Because it has been cultivated for centuries there are many garden hybrids and selected

Plants for dry shade
Ajuga
Alchemilla
Arum
Bergenia
Brunnera
Digitalis
Epimedium
Euphorbia robbiae
Geranium macrorrhizum
Hedera
Helleborus foetidus
Lamium maculatum
Melissa
Pachysandra
Polygonatum
Pulmonaria
Rubus
Symphytum
Tellima
Teucrium
Thalictrum
Tiarella
Vinca
Viola labradorica
Waldsteinia

Galanthus caucasicus

Plants for retentive soil in sun
(Small and low-growing)
Ajuga
Alchemilla conjuncta
Anaphalis triplinervis
Anemone magellanica
Aruncus aethusifolius
Astilbe (dwarf forms)
A. chinensis
A. simplicifolia
Bergenia (dwarf forms)
Camassia esculenta
Campanula burghaltii
C. carpatica turbinata (of gardens)
Colchicum
Epilobium glabellum
Fritillaria verticillata
Geranium (dwarf forms)
Heuchera
× Heucherella
Iris japonica
Myosotis
Omphalodes
Ophiopogon
Parahebe
Polygonum affine 'Superbum'
P. vaccinifolium
Potentilla tabernaemontani
Primula denticulata
Primula vulgaris
Prunella
Ranunculus ficaria 'Flore Plena'
R. speciosus plenus (of gardens)
Sisyrinchium (dwarf forms)
Trifolium
Trollius pumilus
Viola
Waldsteinia

forms. Some require sharp eyes to spot the difference, but enthusiasts have ensured that many beautiful forms are preserved. Single forms may have larger flowers or green-tipped petals, while doubles have tightly packed petals.
10–15cm/4–6in. ZONE 4.

GALTONIA
G. candicans An elegant plant, lovely to cut. Tall stems carry large wax-white bells, like a huge hyacinth. Plant the bulbs in spring. Flowers July until September. It needs sun and good drainage.
120cm/4ft. ZONE 7.
G. princeps Handsome, grey-green broad strap-shaped leaves. Erect stems carry green waxy bells, earlier than G. candicans.
60cm/2ft. ZONE 7.
G. viridiflora Flowers much later than the other two, with heads of wide-open pale-green bells, remarkable in the garden or picked. September to October.
90cm/3ft. ZONE 7.

GAURA
G. lindheimeri Flowers in autumn when there is nothing else like it. Palest-pink flowers float for weeks among graceful branches set with small willow-like leaves. Needs full sun and well-drained soil.
75cm/2½ft. ZONE 5.

GENTIANA
G. asclepiadea The Willow Gentian produces many slender stems clothed with narrow glossy leaves and arched with its weight of true gentian-blue trumpets in early autumn. Does best in full sun and retentive soil.
60cm/2ft. ZONE 5.

GERANIUM
Commonly known as Cranesbills, geraniums are among the most valuable of herbaceous plants, both to fill in between taller plants, or for the singular effects they create when in flower. Among my favourites are the following:
G. cinereum 'Ballerina' This charming small Cranesbill covers the ground with neat mounds of rounded cut greyish foliage. For weeks through summer it produces large crinkled lilac flowers with heavy purple veining and dark centres.

15cm/6in. ZONE 6.
G. dalmaticum Makes low spreading mats of small bronze-tinted shiny leaves, sprinkled with delightful soft rose-pink flowers for weeks in summer.
15cm/6in. ZONE 6.
G. endressii Makes mounds of light apple-green leaves with flowers in varying shades of pink, from June until late autumn.
38cm/15in. ZONE 5.
G. macrorrhizum Flowers in May forming low weed-defeating carpets of scented leaves, some of which turn bright autumn colours while the rest remain all winter. Again there are forms in several shades of pink, from almost white to reddish-purple.
30cm/12in. ZONE 5.
G. psilostemon Forms large leafy plants with magenta-pink flowers with indigo eyes in June.
90cm/3ft. ZONE 6.

Gaura lindheimeri

G. subcaulescens The neat mounds of finely cut leaves – covered with vivid dark-eyed carmine flowers – make a very appealing feature in summer.
23cm/9in. ZONE 6.
G.s. 'Splendens' Its flowers are a lighter, even more stunning shade of carmine-pink than G. subcaulescens, without the dark eyes.
15cm/6in. ZONE 6.
G. sylvaticum 'Album' Large mounds of soft divided leaves; pure white spring flowers.
60cm/2ft. ZONE 6.

GEUM

G. × borisii Makes slowly spreading clumps of rich-green roundish hairy leaves. The single flowers are an unusual shade of rich orange-red, very vivid against the bold foliage in early summer and sometimes again in late summer. Plant in retentive soil in sun.
30cm/1ft. ZONE 7.

GILLENIA

G. trifoliata A graceful plant for semi-shade or full sun in cool retentive soil. Slender russet-coloured stems set with small trifoliate leaves carry sprays of narrow-petalled white flowers which float like moths at dusk in June. When the flowers have gone, reddish-brown calyces remain, quietly attractive for weeks.
90cm/3ft. ZONE 4.

GLADIOLUS

G. papilio Strangely seductive in late summer and autumn. Above narrow, grey-green blade-shaped leaves stand tall stems carrying downcast heads. The slender buds and backs of petals are bruise-shades of green, cream and slate-purple. Inside creamy hearts shelter blue anthers while the lower lip petal is feathered and

Geranium psilostemon with *Artemisia* 'Powis Castle'

marked with an 'eye' in purple and greenish yellow, like the wing of a butterfly. It increases freely. Needs sun and warm well-drained soil.
90cm/3ft. ZONE 8.

GLAUCIUM

G. phoenicium Large rosettes of grey-blue heavily cut leaves; burnt-orange flowers in late summer and autumn are followed by long horn-like pods. Plant in sun in well-drained soil.
60cm/2ft. ZONE 7.

GRASSES

(See pages 62 and 96.)

GRINDELIA

G. chiloensis Branching stems set with narrow curving tooth-edged evergreen leaves are lightly silvered with white dots. In late summer large yellow daisies stand well above foliage on long bare stems, the centre of each opening bud glazed with sticky white, like soft icing sugar. For sunny sheltered spots in well-drained soil, good with greys.
60cm/2ft. ZONE 7.

GUNNERA

(See page 54.)

GYPSOPHILA

G. dubia Ground-hugging mats of green foliage on dark-red stems smothered with white flowers flushed pink. Lovely for a crevice or trailing from a ledge with good drainage and full sun. Flowers from May to June.
8cm/3in. ZONE 5.
G. paniculata 'Rosy Veil' Much bigger. A sight, later in summer or in autumn, with clouds of pale-pink double flowers. It also needs sun and good drainage.
25cm/10in. ZONE 3.

HAPLOPAPPUS

H. coronopifolius Forms a cushion of dark evergreen finely cut foliage studded with sun-loving orange daisy flowers, from August till first frosts. Looks beautiful hanging over a low wall or steps but must have good drainage.
15cm/6in. ZONE 6.

HEDERA

The ivies grow best in part shade and retentive soil.

Plants for retentive soil in sun
(Medium to large)
Achillea decolorans
Alchemilla mollis
Angelica
Aruncus dioicus
Aster
Astrantia
Astilbe taquetii
Bergenia (large forms)
Camassia cusickii
Campanula lactiflora
Centaurea
Chaerophyllum
Chrysanthemum
Echinacea purpurea
Epilobium angustifolium
  'Album'
Euphorbia griffithii
E. longifolia
Gentiana asclepiadea
Geranium (herbaceous types)
Helleborus
Hemerocallis
Houttuynia
Inula
Iris kaempferi
I. sibirica
Kirengeshoma
Knautia
Kniphofia
Libertia
Ligularia
Lobelia
Lysimachia ciliata
L. punctata
Macleaya
Morina
Nerine
Polemonium
Polygonum
Potentilla agyrophylla
Ranunculus acris 'Flore
  Pleno'
Rheum
Rudbeckia
Salvia uliginosa
Schizostylis
Scrophularia
Stachys macrantha
Symphytum caucasicum
Thalictrum aquilegiifolium
Tovara
Trollius europaeus
T. ledebourii (of gardens)
Veratrum
Zigadenus

***H. colchica* 'Sulphur Heart'** ('Paddy's Pride') Has large leaves with a vivid central zone of butter-yellow, softening to palest green at the edges, merging into a strong irregular border of holly-green.
ZONE 6.

H. helix There are many varieties of this, the Common Ivy.

***H. helix* 'Lutzii'** Small prettily mottled leaves in cream, green and primrose.
ZONE 6.

***H. helix poetica* 'Arborea'** Another rarely seen ivy, this is a mature fruiting form which slowly makes a dome-shaped bush and is covered throughout the winter with clusters of fruit which, by spring, have turned a soft orange.
120cm/4ft. ZONE 5.

HELLEBORUS
(See page 84.)

HEMEROCALLIS
These day lilies are easy plants in any soil except the very driest. They thrive in sun or part shade. Their grassy clumps make good ground cover.

H. dumortieri The first Day Lily to make a fine show in early spring. Slender stems carry a wealth of perfumed flowers whose rich yellow petals are accented by dark reddish buds.
60cm/2ft. ZONE 5.

H. flava This lovely species has been grown since the 16th century. Perfect lily-shaped flowers of clear light yellow are very sweetly scented. They flower in early summer and look good among blue or pink cranesbills.
75cm/2½ft. ZONE 5.

HEPATICA
***H. triloba* 'Grandiflora'** I am uncertain of the name for this fine

Heracleum mantegazzianum

form which I found in an old garden. In early spring, its many rich blue petals make flowers the size of a tenpenny piece, smothering the over-wintered leaves; the new leaves continue to make handsome ground cover for the rest of the year. Plant in retentive soil in part shade.
10cm/4in. ZONE 4.

HERACLEUM
H. mantegazzianum The Giant Hogweed stands up to 3m/10ft tall, with huge flat Cow-Parsley-like heads. Best in a mild damp garden. Sap is poisonous.
3m/10ft. ZONE 7.

HEUCHERA
H. americana Quite distinct, it is a beautiful foliage plant that prefers sun or part shade and retentive soil. The new leaves in early spring have a glistening silky texture and are a harmony of warm browns and tan. Strange green and brown flowers in midsummer.
45cm/1½ft. ZONE 4.

***H. cylindrica* 'Greenfinch'** Lovely for picking. Tall well-formed spikes of olive-green bells. Midsummer. This also likes sun or part shade and retentive soil.
75cm/2½ft. ZONE 5.

***H. micrantha diversifolia* 'Palace Purple'** Overlapping heart-shaped leaves with irregularly cut edges are dark bronze-red on the surface, light magenta-pink on the reverse. Faint puckering between the veins accentuates the glistening texture. The flowers are equally beguiling. Masses of wiry dark stems carry feathery heads of tiny white flowers which expand in rosy-bronze seed-pods, all stages to be seen for months from summer to autumn. For not too dry soil in sun or part shade.
45cm/1½ft. ZONE 5.

× HEUCHERELLA
H. × 'Bridget Bloom' Interesting marbled foliage all year round, massed with spikes of light-pink flowers, late spring to early summer. Likes a little shade and humus-fed light soil.
45cm/1½ft. ZONE 3.

HOSTA
(See page 124.)

HOUTTUYNIA
***H. cordata* 'Flore Pleno'** A distinctive plant for cool retentive moist soil or pond-side, it grows in either sun or shade. Elegant heart-shaped leaves shaded with purple are strongly orange-scented, while the pure white double flowers are borne in cone-like clusters. Midsummer.
45cm/1½ft. ZONE 5.

HUMULUS
***H. lupulus* 'Aureus'** The attractive Yellow-leaved Hop. It colours best in full sun or part shade on not too dry retentive soil.
ZONE 3.

INULA
I. magnifica (*afghanica* of gardens) Truly magnificent where there is room to show it off from top to bottom and where it will not be tattered by strong winds. Rough-textured leaves, not unlike dock leaves but far larger, arching and wavy edged ascend stout stems in diminishing size to wide branching heads of large fine-rayed yellow daisies. Splendid in rough grass in retentive soil or by the waterside in full sun. Late summer to early autumn.
2–2.5m/6–8ft. ZONE 5.

IRIS
Although some iris, such as *I. kaempferi*, do need moisture and

sometimes several inches of water (as does *I. laevigata*), others thrive in dry conditions, in either sun or shade. There are many different species and varieties, including some with attractive variegated foliage. The following are just a very brief selection.

I. foetidissima '**Citrina**' Makes strong decorative clumps of tall glossy evergreen leaves. Soft ochre-yellow flowers in June and July, and in November seed-pods that split to reveal hundreds of bright orange seeds.
60cm/2ft. ZONE 6.

I. foetidissima '**Variegata**' Has lovely variegated foliage all year round. Yellow flowers in June and July. It prefers retentive soil and will grow in part shade.
30cm/12in. ZONE 6.

I. japonica The Japanese Iris is a woodland plant, sending up fans of evergreen sword-like leaves from creeping rhizomes. The small, soft lilac-blue flowers are carried in branching sprays. It needs a humus-rich soil and some shelter.
30–60cm/1–2ft. ZONE 7.

I. kaempferi '**Alba**' A particularly attractive pure white form of the Japanese Iris. It flowers in midsummer. Needs damp soil.
45cm/1½ft. ZONE 7.

I. laevigata A handsome waterside plant, which enjoys having its feet in water. The clumps of broad soft green leaves show off the lavender-blue flowers in June.
60cm/2ft. ZONE 7.

I. pallida '**Variegata**' The boldly striped blue-green and white leaves of this variegated iris keep their colour right through the growing season, and are more eye-catching than most flowers. Its own flowers, in June, are light blue. It needs a well-drained sunny border.
45cm/1½ft. ZONE 7.

I. pseudacorus '**Variegata**' A striking variegated form of the Yellow Flag. It grows wild in marshy ground or shallow water but will also grow in rich retentive soil. The yellow flowers have distinct brown markings.
90cm/3ft. ZONE 5.

I. sibirica '**Alba**' A graceful iris, with branching stems of pure white flowers, it will thrive by the waterside or in good ordinary soil. It flowers from June to July.
75cm/2½ft. ZONE 7.

KIRENGESHOMA

K. palmata Needs humus-fed lime-free soil in semi-shade among ferns and hostas. From late summer to autumn, heavy clusters of fat swelling buds open shuttle-cock-shaped flowers about 5cm/2in long, pale butter-yellow and of a thick waxen texture. Irregularly cut maple-like leaves clothe dark purple stems which bow under the weight of flowers. Needs shelter from wind.
90cm/3ft. ZONE 5.

KNAUTIA

K. macedonica (*Scabiosa rumelica*) – what a pity the name cannot remain Scabious because you would recognize it on sight as such! Very free-flowering over a long period, dainty curving stems and branches full of crimson

Iris laevigata
Iris laevigata '**Alba**' (left)

pincushions. Late summer to autumn. Retentive soil and sun. 60cm/2ft. ZONE 8.

KNIPHOFIA

K. 'Green Jade' Forms a medium-sized plant with delicate jade-green flowers. Late summer to autumn. 120cm/4ft. ZONES 7–8.

K. snowdenii A slightly tender Red-hot Poker from Uganda, needing well-drained retentive soil and full sun. Slender stems carry elegant and unusual-looking heads of widely spaced curving flowers in shades of coral, from dark to light. August to November. 90cm/3ft. ZONES 7–8.

LAMIUM

L. maculatum 'Beacon Silver' Makes very good cover in cool soil, part shade. Leaves totally silvered apart from narrow green edging. Has dark pink-lipped flowers in late spring. 10cm/4in. ZONE 3.

L. maculatum 'Shell Pink' This mat-forming Dead Nettle with its beautifully frosted green and white leaves makes excellent ground cover and delights everyone with shell-pink flowers in early summer. 15cm/6in. ZONE 3.

L. maculatum 'White Nancy' Another silver-leaved form that has ivory-white flowers in early summer. 13cm/5in. ZONE 3.

LATHYRUS

L. latifolius 'White Pearl' A perennial pea producing sprays of pure white scentless but beautifully formed flowers. I let it scramble through old-fashioned roses and pick it for weeks in midsummer to put in little mixed bowls. It needs full sun and retentive soil. Up to 120cm/4ft. ZONE 5.

L. vernus roseus Forms a bushy little plant with many stems bearing neat divided leaves. In April it is covered with tiny rose-pink pea flowers. For sun or semi-shade in not too dry retentive soil. 30cm/1ft. ZONE 5.

LAVANDULA

L. angustifolia 'Loddon Pink' Spikes of dusty-pink flowers in June to July, over compact bushes of narrow grey-green leaves. For sunny well-drained areas. 38–60cm/15–24in. ZONE 7.

L. angustifolia 'Nana Alba' Dwarf compact bushes with comparatively broad grey-green leaves, carrying heads of white flowers in July. 30cm/1ft. ZONE 7.

L. stoechas A compact little bush covered in mid- to late summer with curious knobbly flower-heads which carry two kinds of flowers. The fertile flowers arranged in vertical rows are small and very dark purple-blue. Above them, to entice pollinating insects, is a 'flag' of large wavy petals in a lighter shade of purple. It needs very well-drained soil. 38cm/15in. ZONE 8.

L. stoechas pedunculatus This is distinguished by much longer 'flags' or 'ears' of rose-pink. It has survived two severe winters in my garden in well-drained soil. 38cm/15in. ZONE 8.

LEUCANTHEMUM

L. hosmariense Finely fingered clusters of silver-grey leaves make a comfortably low mound, carrying in winter hundreds of tight black-pencilled buds which open a few large white daisies in mild spells and make a glorious show in spring and early summer. Needs full sun and good drainage. 30cm/1ft. ZONE 5.

LIBERTIA

L. formosa Narrow evergreen iris-like foliage forms dense tufts above which rise long slender spikes of small ivory-white flowers in July, followed by brown bobbly

Kniphofia snowdenii

Kniphofia hybrids

seed-heads. Grows best in sun and needs good drainage.
75cm/2½ft. ZONE 8.

L. grandiflora Beautiful species with tall spikes of large three-petalled flowers in pure white. Safer in a warm border in well-drained soil with a little peat.
75cm/2½ft. ZONE 8.

LIGULARIA

L. clivorum 'Desdemona' For moist-retentive soil and full sun, having large heart-shaped leaves, bronze-purple above with bright magenta backs; big, branching heads of orange-rayed flowers appear in late summer.
120cm/4ft. ZONE 3.

L. 'Gregynog Gold' Most noble feature plant for damp soil or the waterside. Forms mounds of large heart-shaped leaves above which tower great clustered spikes of rich yellow daisy flowers. Mid- to late summer.
2m/6ft. ZONE 3.

L. stenocephala 'The Rocket' Forms a fine mound of large round leaves with serrated edges. Tall, almost black stems standing well above the leaves carry long cylindrical spires of small bright yellow flowers, making a distinguished vertical feature in damp soil in late summer.
1.5m/5ft. ZONE 3.

LILIUM

L. martagon Also known as Turk's Cap Lily. Tall stems crowded with soft pinkish-purple flowers in midsummer. It needs full sun or part shade and a deep soil. There is also a white form, *L.m.* 'Album'.
1–1.2m/3–4ft. ZONE 6.

L. speciosum The flowers, produced in August and September, vary in colour from white to deep rose pink. Does best in rich soil.
1.2–1.5m/4–5ft. ZONE 6.

LINARIA

L. purpurea 'Canon Went' A tall delicate Toadflax, carrying spires of tiny pale-pink flowers throughout the summer. For sunny areas with good drainage.
75cm/2½ft. ZONE 7.

L. triornithophora This means 'bearing three birds' – its buds look like tiny budgerigars. It has purple or occasionally pink flowers all summer long until the first frosts. Needs sun and soil with good drainage.
90cm/3ft. ZONE 7.

LINUM

L. flavum 'Compactum' Neat shrubby plants covered with rosettes of fresh green leaves carry branched heads of cool yellow flowers in midsummer. Plant in well-drained soil in sun.
30–38cm/12–15in. ZONE 5.

L. salsoloides 'Prostratum' A captivating plant for a rock garden or raised bed. Prostrate stems clothed in tiny narrow blue-grey leaves form a flat carpet embroidered with shallow funnel-shaped flowers in white, lightly pencilled with purple. Midsummer. Needs sun and good drainage.
2.5cm/1in. ZONE 6.

LIPPIA

L. citriodora Long slender branches bear deliciously lemon-scented leaves (hence the common name, Lemon Verbena): they can be dried to make herb tea or pot-pourri. The panicles of tiny violet and white flowers in August are not without charm. Needs shelter of a warm wall, full sun and good drainage. Normally cut down by severe winters, but shoots again next spring.
120cm/4ft stems in one season. ZONE 8.

LOBELIA

L. cardinalis 'Queen Victoria' A startling plant for damp retentive soil and sun, best covered in mulch in late autumn until last frosts of spring have gone, which can damage emerging shoots. Beetroot-red leaves combine with brilliantly scarlet flowers.
75cm/2½ft. ZONE 2.

LYSICHITUM

Both species here make superb bog garden plants but need time to establish into flowering plants.

L. americanum This Bog Arum must have deep rich mud and full sun. Then, in spring, it delights with its thick yellow spathes unfolding first, followed by magnificent huge leaves, making an architectural feature throughout the summer.
120cm/4ft. ZONE 6.

L. camtschatcense From Siberia and Japan comes a pure white-flowered species.
Foliage 90cm/3ft. ZONE 5.

LYSIMACHIA

L. ciliata Emerges through the soil in spring with clusters of soft milk-chocolate-brown leaves whose colour is only slightly diluted green as the stems elongate to carry a spire of delicately hung yellow flowers which last for weeks in mid- to late summer. Creeping rootstock in rich to damp soil in sun.
75cm/2½ft. ZONE 4.

L. nummularia 'Aurea' Delightful ground cover in cool retentive soil and part shade, this Creeping Jenny has bright gold foliage and shallow saucer-shaped yellow flowers in midsummer.
5cm/2in. ZONE 3.

L. punctata Can be seen anywhere from ditchside to seemingly dry front garden, but for semi-wild planting it needs sun and damp

Ligularia × palmatiloba

Lilium martagon '**Album**'

retentive soil – it can then be invasive. Spires of bright yellow flowers mid- to late summer. 90cm/3ft. ZONE 5.

LYTHRUM

L. salicaria 'Robert' Makes a fine feature plant with branching spikes of small rose-pink flowers. Will grow in any good retentive soil, including the bog garden, but needs sun. Late summer to autumn.
120cm/4ft. ZONE 3.
L. virgatum 'Rose Queen' Makes a small tapering branched plant ablaze in late summer with rosy-pink flowers which practically hide the small narrow leaves. Needs soil that does not dry out. 60cm/2ft. ZONE 4.

MACLEAYA

M. microcarpa 'Coral Plume' A statuesque plant, either in isolation or in a bay among shrubs. For full sun and retentive soil. A running rootstock throws up many tall strong stems which need no staking. Large rounded, deeply indented leaves are grey-green above, grey-white beneath. Long branching plumes of small pale apricot buds open to rich-cream fluffy flowers. Later summer to autumn.
2m/7ft. ZONE 3.

MALVA

M. moschata 'Alba' Covered in silky-white saucer-shaped flowers, this pretty Mallow causes comment for weeks in summer. Seeds itself usefully. Best in sun and well-drained soil.
45cm/1½ft. ZONE 3.

MELISSA

M. officinalis 'Aurea' Has rich-yellow matt-textured leaves from beginning of season to the very end. It needs good drainage and partial shade to prevent leaf scorch on its delicately lovely foliage. Insignificant flowers. 60cm/2ft. ZONE 4.

MITELLA

M. breweri Rounded, scallop-edged dark green leaves, arranged in neat clumps. In spring, tiny forests of pale leafless stems carry wands of minute green flowers with fringed edges. Charming on the edge of a shady path but must be in retentive soil.
17cm/7in. ZONE 4.
M. caulescens A delight in awkward shade. Thread-like stems run over the soil, forming carpets or edgings of pea-green heart-shaped leaves, with tiny palest-green flowers in spring. 8cm/3in. ZONE 4.

MORINA

M. longifolia A most distinctive plant for full sun and retentive soil. Forms rosettes of prickly aromatic foliage, from which rise tall stems, bearing pagoda-like chalices, set at intervals. These are packed with jade-green tubes from which spring white tubular flowers changing to crimson with age. After the flowers are finished the standing green stem with its fantastic outline is perhaps even more beautiful for green arrangements. Effective midsummer to winter.
75cm/2½ft. ZONE 5.

MYOSOTIS

M. scorpioides (*palustris*) **'Mermaid'** Different from the spreading common Water Forget-me-not, this plant is very compact, covered with short-stemmed blue flowers for weeks in summer. It flourishes in retentive rich soil and full sun. 5–8cm/2–3in. ZONE 3.

NARCISSUS

N. minor 'Cedric Morris' This unique daffodil is usually in flower for Christmas Day, continuing to bloom through the worst of weathers till March. Small lemon-yellow perfectly formed daffodils with lightly frilled trumpets, a joy to pick with early snowdrops. Plant in shade to protect from Narcissus Fly. Needs retentive soil.
15–30cm/6–12in. ZONE 5.

NERINE

N. bowdenii Glorious pink trumpets in October. Winters well under a warm wall, or in very well-drained soil. For full sun. 30–38cm/12–15in. ZONE 7.

OMPHALODES

O. cappadocica Forms dense clumps of oval, slightly crinkled green leaves over which float sprays of intense gentian-blue flowers, larger than those of Forget-me-not. Breath-taking in spring, a few nostalgic reminders in autumn. A very good ground cover in retentive soil.
23cm/9in. ZONE 5.

OPHIOPOGON

O. planiscapus nigrescens Arching strap-shaped leaves make spidery clusters against the soil, a feature all year round and remarkable because they are black. In summer, short sprays of tiny mauve bells appear, maturing as shiny black berries which last well into winter. Creeps slowly in well-drained but retentive soil, in sun or part shade.
25cm/10in. ZONE 8.

PACHYPHRAGMA

P. macrophylla (*Cardamine asarifolia*) To see under trees and shrubs an established carpet of

Plants for damp shade
(Small and low-growing)
Ajuga
Alchemilla conjuncta
Arum
Aruncus aethusifolius
Astilbe (dwarf forms)
Chrysanthemum parthenium
Dentaria digitata
Disporum
Epilobium glabellum
Epimedium
Erythronium
Fritillaria camtschatcensis
Hepatica
× *Heucherella*
Lamium
Lysimachia nummularia
Mitella
Narcissus minor 'Cedric Morris'
Omphalodes
Pachysandra
Phlox stolonifera
Polygonum affine 'Superbum'
P. vaccinifolium
Primula pulverulenta
P. vulgaris
Pulmonaria
Saxifraga
Symphytum grandiflorum
Tellima
Tiarella
Uvularia perfoliata
Viola
Waldsteinia

these large round green leaves overlapping to make weed-free cover is very pleasant all summer. Veins and stems become purple-tinted in winter. As snowdrops fade showy heads of white cress-like flowers appear early in March before new leaves. Does not run and can be divided. It prefers shade and retentive soil. 30cm/1ft. ZONE 5.

PACHYSANDRA

P. terminalis Most valued rich green carpeter for covering bare earth beneath trees or shrubs. It grows well in shade and retentive soil. Evergreen rosettes of toothed glossy leaves, insignificant white scented flowers in spring. 30cm/1ft. ZONE 4.

PAEONIA

P. 'Avant Garde' Given me by Eric Smith. A delicate-looking peony with enchanting pink flowers. 75cm/30in. ZONE 6.
P. mlokosewitschii In early spring the buds and young leaves are a rich pinkish-bronze. As they turn to soft grey-green the buds gradually open to full beauty, perfect bowls of cool lemon-yellow, filled with golden stamens in May. For part shade and retentive soil. 60cm/2ft. ZONE 5.

PARAHEBE

P. catarractae 'Alba' An excellent plant for sunny areas and retentive soil. Tidy mound of evergreen leaves, completely whitened like snow by the thousands of tiny 'bird's-eye' flowers in early summer. 15cm/6in. ZONE 6.

PELTIPHYLLUM

P. peltatum In early spring tall, naked stems appear from thick, flattish rhizomes, carrying flat

heads of pale pink flowers. Scallop-edged, parasol-shaped leaves, up to 30cm/12in across follow. For damp soil in sun. 60–75cm/2–2½ft. ZONE 5.

PENSTEMON

P. barbatus (*Chelone barbata*) Spreads flat rosettes of narrow green leaves. Surprisingly tall slender branching stems shoot up carrying bright-scarlet, narrow tubular flowers. Hardy on well-drained soil in sun. Late summer.
90cm/3ft. ZONE 3.
P. 'Evelyn' Forms neat bush plants of very narrow leaves topped with slender spires of slim flowers, rose-pink with pale striped throats. In flower all summer. Needs well-drained soil and sun. 60cm/2ft. ZONE 3.

PEROVSKIA

P. atriplicifolia 'Blue Spire' Makes a feature as soon as the slender whitened stems, lightly clad in fine-cut grey leaves, appear above the surrounding mounds. In late summer they are topped with long spires of lavender-blue flowers. Needs sun and good drainage. 120cm/4ft. ZONE 6.

PETASITES

P. japonicus giganteus While flower-arrangers love the posy-like heads of green and white flowers which burst through bare clay in early spring, this is a plant for landscaping with its huge round leaves and invasive roots, making impenetrable ground cover in heavy retentive soil in sun or part shade. 120–150cm/4–5ft. ZONE 4.

Plants for damp shade
(Medium to large)
Alchemilla mollis
Angelica
Aruncus dioicus
Astilbe taquetii
Astrantia
Bergenia
Brunnera
Cimicifuga
Dicentra spectabilis
Digitalis
Gentiana asclepiadea
Hedera
Helleborus
Hosta
Humulus lupulus
Ligularia
Lysimachia
Pachyphragma
Paeonia mlokosewitschii
Polygonatum
Polygonum
Rheum
Rodgersia
Scrophularia
Smilacina
Trachystemon
Veratrum
Zantedeschia
Zigadenus

Paeonia 'Avant Garde'

Plants for clay soils

Acanthus
Alchemilla
Aruncus
Bergenia
Brunnera
Caltha
Epimedium
Euphorbia robbiae
Geranium
Hedera
Helleborus
Hemerocallis
Hosta
Inula
Lamium
Peltiphyllum
Petasites
Polygonum
Primula denticulata
P. vulgaris
Prunella
Rheum
Rodgersia
Saxifraga caucasicus
Saxifraga × urbium
Symphytum
Trachystemon
Vinca
Waldsteinia

PHLOMIS

P. russeliana (*samia, viscosa* of gardens) From large weed-smothering clumps of soft heart-shaped leaves rise stiff stems carrying whorls of rich-yellow hooded flowers in midsummer. The seed-heads, whether green or dried, are equally effective. For sun and retentive soil. 90cm/3ft. ZONE 7.

PHLOX

P. stolonifera 'Ariane' The prostrate forms of *Phlox* are a delight both for their weed-suppressing habit and for their flowers, beautiful individually or in breath-taking sheets of colour. Spreading mats of light green leaves are a background for loose heads of snow-white yellow-eyed flowers. Best in part shade and retentive soil. April to May. 20cm/8in. ZONE 4.

P. stolonifera 'Blue Ridge' Prefers cool conditions, semi-shade and a little peat. It makes good ground cover, above which stand heads of lilac-blue flowers with a pin-eye of orange stamens. April to May. 20cm/8in. ZONE 4.

PHYTOLACCA

P. americana The Virginian Poke Weed sends up each year from a huge mangold-like root a stout plant with thick branching stems ending in a spike of close-packed white flowers which turn into shining maroon berries. Flowers midsummer. Needs sun and retentive soil. 120cm/4ft. ZONE 3.

P. clavigera From China. Very similar in shape, this has bright rose-pink flowers followed by elderberry-black berries, contrasting with rhubarb-red stems and yellow autumn foliage. 120cm/4ft. ZONE 3.

POLEMONIUM

P. caeruleum Also known as Jacob's Ladder. Held well above clumps of fresh green divided foliage are an endless succession of sky-blue small open bells, orange-centred. Charming, especially in a cool situation where it has sun and retentive soil; early to midsummer. 60cm/2ft. ZONE 3.

P. caeruleum 'Album' A good white form, in flower for weeks,

from late spring to late summer. 60cm/2ft. ZONE 4.

P. carneum In early summer produces sheaves of silky pearl-pink cupped flowers, lovely as an edging plant. 45cm/1½ft. ZONE 4.

POLYGONATUM

P. × hybridum (*P. multiflorum* of gardens) This is the usual form of Solomon's Seal. Close-set spreading rhizomes send up tall arching stems set with shining dark green leaves. In May they bear white and green-flushed bells on the lower side of the leafy shoots. For planting in shade or part shade in retentive soil. 75–90cm/2½–3ft. ZONE 4.

P. × hybridum 'Variegatum' This seldom seen form has leaves boldly striped and edges creamy-white. 60cm/2ft. ZONE 4.

P. multiflorum Distinct from *P. × hybridum*. Shorter, more upright stems hold leaves more closely set, standing upright on top side of slightly arched stems to show wax-blue undersides. Beneath hang small cream bells followed by berries, at first dark bloom-coated green, finally almost black. 60cm/2ft. ZONE 4.

POLYGONUM

P. affine 'Suberbum' Low spreading mats of neat green leaves, which turn rich russet-brown in autumn and remain all winter. Spikes of pale pink flowers from midsummer to autumn. 23cm/9in. ZONE 6.

P. amplexicaule 'Album' Slim tapers of tiny white flowers smother tall bushy plants for months. Needs sun and retentive soil. 120cm/4ft. ZONE 6.

P. amplexicaule 'Atrosanguineum' Forms large branching bushy

Phlox stolonifera 'Ariane'

178

plants which glow with slender tapers of tiny crimson flowers all late summer and autumn. 120cm/4ft. ZONE 6.

P. bistorta 'Superbum' Best in a moist soil. Massed stems carry thick cyclamen-pink pokers; handsome dock-like foliage. Early summer. 75cm/2½ft. ZONE 3.

P. vaccinifolium This plant leafs very late in spring when its mats of russet-brown stems push out tiny shining green leaves. By late September it is smothered with spikes of tiny pink flowers. 8cm/3in. ZONE 6.

PONTEDERIA

P. cordata The handsome Pickerel Weed spreads slowly out into shallow water from the boggy edge. Standing above the water are crowded stems of beautiful leaves, spear-shaped, marked with faint swirling lines and shadows, all topped with spikes of small blue flowers in late summer. 45cm/1½ft above water. ZONE 5.

POTENTILLA

P. alba Useful ground cover for sun or light shade in retentive soil, formed by mats of soft grey-green lupin-like leaves, which are covered with orange-eyed white flowers in spring and again in autumn. 10cm/4in. ZONE 6.

P. argyrophylla Neat clumps of heavily silvered strawberry-like leaves are a base for branching sprays of yellow flowers with orange centres for many weeks in midsummer. Best in sun and retentive soil. 45cm/1½ft. ZONE 5.

P. tabernaemontani 'Goldrausch' A superb plant. Neat mats of small dark-green leaves are edged with short sprays of bright yellow

flowers like a doily. From spring until November frosts. 5–8cm/2–3in. ZONE 6.

PRIMULA

P. denticulata 'Alba' Beautiful form, white flowers, yellow eyes with large rosettes of luscious pale-green leaves. Spring. For full sun and retentive soil. 30cm/1ft. ZONE 5.

P. pulverulenta Deep wine-coloured flowers with purple eyes. A favourite bog primula for damp, shady soil. 60cm/2ft. ZONE 5.

P. vulgaris 'Alba' Close-packed stems of ivory-white yellow-eyed primroses surrounded by a ruff of green crinkled leaves. 15cm/6in. ZONE 3.

PRUNELLA

P. webbiana 'Loveliness' Short dense spikes of pale-violet flowers in midsummer, shaped like Dead Nettle. Good edging plant, or

Pontederia cordata (left)

Primula vulgaris 'Alba' (above)

Primula pulverulenta and *P.p.* 'Bartley Strain' (pale pink)

makes useful ground cover for sun and retentive soil. 15cm/6in. ZONE 6.

PULMONARIA

Also known as Lungwort, pulmonarias make excellent ground cover in moisture-retaining soil, preferring partial shade. They are among the first plants to flower, regardless of weather. There is considerable variation, both from interbred seedlings and varying clones.

P. longifolia The flat basal rosettes form an eye-catching star-shape against the soil, each dark-green white-spotted leaf being long and narrow, tapering to a point. Rich blue flowers in dense terminal clusters. The latest to flower, into summer.
30cm/1ft. ZONE 4.

P. officinalis 'Cambridge Blue' This is an especially good form of the well-known Lungwort, often called Soldiers and Sailors or Spotted Dog. Heart-shaped spotted leaves, much smaller than those of *P. saccharata* are lost in early spring below the haze of light blue flowers, opening from faint pink buds.
25cm/10in. ZONE 3.

P. rubra Weed-smothering clumps of large light-green leaves, unspotted, are preceded in very early spring by clustered heads of coral-red tubular flowers.
30cm/1ft. ZONE 5.

P. saccharata Not the common Lungwort. These leaves are up to 30cm/1ft long, rough-textured, dark green, variously marbled in silver and grey-green. Most striking in shady corners. Likes cool soil. Masses of blue and rose-coloured flowers in March.
30cm/1ft. ZONE 3.

P. saccharata 'Alba' This fine form produces quantities of snow-white large pearl-sized flowers followed by rosettes of well-marked leaves for the rest of the season.
30cm/1ft. ZONE 3.

P. saccharata 'Argentea' A large clump of these frosted-silver leaves under the shade of shrubs is a lovely sight. Flowers in March.
30cm/1ft. ZONE 3.

RANUNCULUS

R. acris 'Flore Pleno' Deserves to be better known. Almost leafless branching stems carry multitudes of small tightly double buttercups, lovely among blue *Iris sibirica*. All *Ranunculus* like retentive soil and sun. June to July.
90cm/3ft. ZONE 3.

R. ficaria 'Flore Plena' This is a double celandine, very attractive with tightly packed petals of glistening yellow, green-centred when young in April.
8cm/3in. ZONE 5.

R. speciosus plenus (of gardens) Non-invasive, a choice plant for damp retentive soil in sun, it produces many large tightly double, glossy yellow flowers, sharply green-centred. Early summer.
30cm/1ft. ZONE 5.

RHEUM

R. palmatum This plant is worthy of a place in the wild garden or in a

Rheum palmatum

bay in a shrubbery. The first year will see a huge weed-smothering mound of apple-green leaves that are 1m/3ft across. Stout flower-stems carry branched heads of frothy white flowers in June. For sun or part shade and retentive soil.
2m/6ft. ZONE 6.

R. palmatum 'Atrosanguineum' When young its crinkled leaves are rosy-purple, the topsides later turning dark green. Tall branching spires are massed with tiny cherry-red flowers in early summer, producing translucent rose-red seed-cases. Needs plenty of humus.
2m/6ft. ZONE 6.

RODGERSIA

These are among the finest foliage plants for marshy land, waterside or cool, damp retentive soil. Will grow in sun if soil is moist, also in shade provided soil does not dry out. They make slowly spreading rhizomes.

R. podophylla The young unfolding leaves are rich dark brown in spring, turning green as they expand, often copper-tinted when mature. Each dramatically handsome leaf consists of five large leaflets, broadly triangular in outline, with jagged tips, arranged at the top of each stem. The head of

Seed-heads
Acanthus
Achillea
Agapanthus
Allium
Anaphalis
Aruncus
Asphodelus
Ballota
Baptisia
Carlina
Crocosmia
Cynara
Digitalis
Eryngium
Galtonia
Heuchera
Hosta
Iris sibirica
Lythrum virgatum
Malva moschata
Morina
Phlomis russeliana
Thalictrum aquilegiifolium
Verbascum pulverulentum
Zigadenus

Pulmonaria rubra (top)

Pulmonaria longifolia
with P. saccharata

creamy astilbe-like flowers is not remarkable.
60cm/2ft. ZONE 4.

R. tabularis Differs in having large round simple leaves, the size and shape of a dinner-plate (or a tea-tray in very good moist soil), dimpled in the centre. The leaf edges are slightly scalloped. One of the most beautiful and calming of leaves for a shady place. A strong flower-stem carries heavy drooping clusters of star-shaped creamy-white flowers in late summer.
90cm/3ft. ZONE 5.

RUBUS

R. idaeus 'Aureus' A form of raspberry. Very attractive plant for part shade and retentive soil, where there is room, among shrubs, or in the leaf litter beneath trees. Pale lemon-yellow leaves create a patch of sunlight where its underground shoots weave through fine leaf-mould.
25–38cm/10–15in. ZONE 5.

R. thibetanus A 'ghost' bramble. Lovely in winter and summer. A small forest of totally whitened stems, 90–120cm/3–4ft tall, springs from the soil, branching and bending gracefully to present – almost horizontally to the light – pretty frosted-looking leaves, soft grey-green above, whitened beneath. ZONE 6.

R. tricolor Beautiful evergreen ground cover where something rampant can be appreciated. Prostrate stems covered with soft reddish hairs carry shining polished green leaves which become bronze-tinted with purplish margins.
Makes over 2m/6ft of growth in a season. ZONE 7.

RUDBECKIA

R. fulgida (*speciosa, newmanii*) Making a bright display in autumn,

this very tidy daisy forms mounds of dark-green foliage to set off large bright-yellow flowers, each with a prominent black eye. For sunny areas and retentive soil.
60cm/2ft. ZONE 3.

R. fulgida 'Deamii' Considered to be an improved form; similar, slightly taller, rougher foliage. Late summer to autumn.
75cm/2½ft. ZONE 3.

RUMEX

R. hydrolapathum Also known as 'the Great Water Dock. A striking plant for large pools. The smooth large fairly narrow leaves sometimes turn red in autumn. Brownish-pink flowers in late summer.
1.5m/5ft. ZONE 6.

RUTA

R. graveolens 'Jackman's Blue' Neat mounds of blue filigree foliage. Evergreen. Lovely under old-fashioned roses, with *Alchemilla mollis* or grey plants. Its small yellow flowers are of little merit. For sunny areas.
45cm/1½ft. ZONE 5.

SALVIA

S. blancoana In sun and well-drained soil, this choice sage makes a low spreading bush covered with narrow silver-grey leaves. From the tip shoots extend long curving sprays of soft lilac-blue flowers in midsummer.
30cm/1ft. ZONE 5.

S. nemorosa 'Superba' Clumps of rich green crêpy leaves send up stiff spikes of intense violet-purple flowers with crimson bracts in mid- to late summer.
90cm/3ft. ZONE 5.

S. officinalis 'Purpurascens' The young summer foliage of Purple Sage is a delight, soft greyish-purple velvet, with spikes of

Rumex hydrolapathum

purple-blue flowers in early summer. Occasional shoots are variegated pink, cream and purple. Will form a lax bush, but can be kept under control by careful pruning in spring. Needs sun and good drainage.
60cm/2ft. ZONE 6.

S. uliginosa Worth protecting underground shoots with a bit of bracken or straw. In late September slender leafy stems carry head-high loose spires of pure sky-blue flowers. Needs a warm sunny site, yet soil that does not dry out.
1.5m/5ft. ZONE 8.

SANTOLINA

S. virens (*viridis*) Drought-resisting, yet green, useful as contrast among silver plants in sunny, well-drained areas. Forms a neat round bush of vivid green aromatic foliage, a bright setting for the lemon-yellow button flowers. Midsummer.
45cm/1½ft. ZONE 7.

SAXIFRAGA

S. × urbium 'Aurea Punctata' (*S. umbrosa* 'Variegata') Also known as London Pride. Richly variegated gold and green. Sprays of pale pink flowers in early summer. For part-shade and retentive soil.
23cm/9in. ZONE 6.

Rodgersia podophylla

SCABIOSA

S. caucasica 'Miss Willmott' In flower for months throughout the summer. Large pale-cream, almost greenish-white flowers on tall stems are produced endlessly till the frosts.
75cm/2½ft. ZONE 3.

SCHIZOSTYLIS

S. coccinea 'Major' Also known as Kaffir Lily. Makes spreading patches of grassy-leaved shoots which send up slender spires of slim buds. Throughout autumn and mild days in winter they open glistening shallow cups, jewel-like and cherry-red. They need retentive soil and moisture all summer but also warmth and sun to encourage early flowering.
38cm/15in. ZONE 8.
S. 'Sunrise' Large salmon-pink flowers open in October and continue into December.
38cm/15in. ZONE 8.

Schizostylis 'Sunrise'

SCROPHULARIA

S. aquatica 'Variegata' The Variegated Water Figwort makes a spectacular foliage plant in sun or part shade. Its broad basal leaves are waved and crimpled and richly banded in cream, the centre shaded in greens. The smaller leaves in branching stems are also variegated, sometimes totally cream. Needs rich retentive soil.
60cm/2ft. ZONE 6.

SEDUM

S. 'Autumn Joy' From icy-looking clumps of fleshy leaves sturdy stems are topped with dense flat heads packed with brick-red stars. They flower from late summer, remaining handsome until the frosts. Need sun and good drainage.
45cm/1½ft. ZONE 3.
S. spectabile 'Brilliant' Large flat heads of bright mauve-pink flowers, humming with bees, in late summer.
45cm/1½ft. ZONE 3.
S. spurium 'Green Mantle' Makes solid ground cover, creeping stems carrying close-packed rosettes of broad green leaves.
13cm/5in. ZONE 3.

SEMPERVIVUM

Some grow as wide across as a saucer, making handsome feature plants for sunny, well-drained areas. Others are tiny, suitable for sink trough gardens or crevices in the rock-garden. Among the larger ones the texture is mostly waxen or smooth as marble, apple-green rosettes tipped with mahogany, shadowed with purple, or glowing bronze-red. The small ones are also found in warm shades of bronze and mahogany. But there are also the 'cobweb'-covered forms, and those with incurved leaves edged with bristly hairs. To look down on to my stock beds of all these sempervivums arranged in square blocks is somewhat reminiscent of mosaic paving, as each rosette makes a ring of youngsters around it and the soil becomes completely covered. There are many species and named hybrids. ZONE 5.

Sempervivum beta

SENECIO

S. smithii A sun-loving plant for moist soil, or shallow water by pond edges or in bogs. Huge basal leaves, broadly spear-shaped, glossy green, puckered and tooth-edged, greyish beneath. They ascend thick stems topped in midsummer with densely clustered flower-heads, sometimes 30cm/1ft across, of yellow-eyed white daisies. Fluffy seed-heads follow.
120cm/4ft. ZONE 6.

SIDERITIS

S. syriacus For warm, sunny, well-drained gardens – not suited to winter wet. Low woody stems support rosettes of white woolly leaves from which emerge in midsummer long, graceful flower heads with small lemon-yellow flowers tucked in among white 'cotton wool'.
25–30cm/10–12in. ZONE 8.

SISYRINCHIUM

S. angustifolium Also known as Blue-Eyed Grass. Clumps of little grassy leaves are topped in midsummer by satiny deep-blue flowers clustered on short stems. Needs sun and retentive soil.
10cm/4in. ZONE 3.
S. idahoense Impressive, with good-sized deep-blue flowers on erect stems, produced for weeks on end in midsummer.
25cm/10in. ZONE 7.
S. 'Quaint 'n' Queer' (*nudicaule × montanum*) Curiously attractive chocolate and cream flowers spangle stiff branching, sprawling stems for months, throughout midsummer and into autumn.
38cm/15in. ZONE 7.

SMILACINA

S. racemosa Related to Solomon's Seal and very like it in its beautiful arching foliage, but instead of bells

Smilacina racemosa

it has a tapering head of massed fluffy, creamy-white flowers sweetly scented. Late spring. Likes cool retentive soil and part shade. 75cm/2½ft. ZONE 3.

STACHYS

S. macrantha (*Betonica grandiflora*) Makes slowly spreading clumps of rich green, scallop-edged leaves, while rosy-mauve funnel-shaped flowers in whorls are held on erect branching stems in June. A lovely plant for retentive soil and full sun. 60cm/2ft. ZONE 3.

SYMPHYTUM

S. caucasicum Clusters of grey-green pointed leaves colonize by underground stems, horribly invasive in the wrong place, but where allowable it is one of the delights of spring, with arching stems carrying clusters of sky-blue tubular flowers. Best in retentive soil in sun or part shade. 60cm/2ft. ZONE 3.

S. grandiflorum This is a most useful and handsome plant making impenetrable weed-cover in retentive soil in shade among shrubs. It forms mounds of large dark-green leaves, spreading by underground shoots. In spring before the new leaves are fully developed the fiddle-neck clusters of flowers change from orange buds to creamy-yellow bells. 30cm/1ft. ZONE 3.

TELLIMA

T. grandiflora 'Odorata' Scented form. Foliage not so deeply coloured in winter as that of the following form, but the flowers smell deliciously of old-fashioned pinks, scenting the air for yards around. Both need retentive soil in sun or part shade. 60cm/2ft. ZONE 4.

T. grandiflora 'Purpurea' An all-the-year-round foliage plant. Spreading clumps of round scalloped leaves, green above, purple beneath, changing to rich red-purples and bronze in winter. In early summer there are tall spikes of pink-fringed green bells. 60cm/2ft. ZONE 4.

THALICTRUM

T. aquilegiifolium From a basal clump of grey-green leaves, finely divided, slender purple stems ascend carrying pretty fans of leaves, topped with large heads of fluffy, rosy-lilac flowers. Early to midsummer. Likes sun and retentive soil. Seed-heads are good green or dried. 90–120cm/3–4ft. ZONE 5.

THYMUS

T. herba barona Caraway-scented form. Wiry mats of dark green leaves heavily scented of caraway seeds. Pink and mauve flowers. Needs sun and good drainage. 10cm/4in. ZONE 4.

T. herba barona Lemon-scented form. Collected in Corsica. 10cm/4in. ZONE 4.

TIARELLA

All tiarellas need humus-rich soil in part shade.

T. collina Makes neat clumps of white starry flowers in May. 30cm/12in. ZONE 3.

Tiarella collina

Handsome foliage plants
Acanthus
Acorus
Ajuga
Alchemilla
Artemisia
Arum italicum 'Pictum'
Astrantia major 'Sunningdale Variety'
Ballota
Bergenia
Brunnera
Crambe
Cynara
Disporum sessile 'Variegatum'
Epimedium
Eryngium agavifolium
Euphorbia
Geranium
Glaucium phoenicium
Grindelia
Gunnera
Hedera
Helleborus
Heuchera
Hosta
Lamium
Libertia
Ligularia
Lysichitum
Lysimachia nummularia 'Aurea'
Onopordum
Ophiopogon
Peltiphyllum
Polygonatum
Pulmonaria
Rheum palmatum
Rodgersia
Rubus
Salvia officinalis 'Purpurascens'
Saxifraga × urbium
Scrophularia aquatica 'Variegata'
Sedum
Sideritis
Stachys
Symphytum grandiflorum
Tellima grandiflora
Tovara
Trachystemon
Trifolium repens 'Purpurascens Quadriphyllum'
Verbascum pulverulentum
Vinca
Viola labradorica
Zantedeschia

Verbascum chaixii 'Album'

Plants attractive to butterflies
Achillea
Anaphalis
Ajuga
Aster
Calamintha
Chrysanthemum rubellum
Dianthus deltoides
Echinacea
Erigeron
Knautia
Ligularia
Lysimachia
Melissa
Phlox
Polygonum
Primula
Scabiosa
Sedum spectabile 'Brilliant'
Thymus herba-barona
Verbena bonariensis

T. cordifolia Running trails of pretty pointed green leaves form complete cover in spring. A mass of foaming creamy-white flower spikes in early summer. Grows in part shade.
23–30cm/9–12in. ZONE 3.
T. wherryi This also has delicate spires of starry white flowers, but the leaves are like shadowed green velvet; exquisite for months. Midsummer.
25cm/10in. ZONE 3.

TOVARA

T. filiformis 'Painter's Palette' Forms low branching plants covered with large oval leaves marbled in shades of cream and green, faintly brushed with pink. The centre of each leaf is marked with a strong 'V'. Tiny rat-tail wisps of little brown flowers show its relationship with *Polygonum*. For sun or part shade and good soil.
60cm/2ft. ZONE 8.
T. virginiana 'Variegata' Is very like *T. filiformis* 'Painter's Palette', but without the 'V' mark and flushes of pink. It makes a beautiful cool feature among plain green companions in retentive soil. Both forms need shelter from sun scorch and wind.
60cm/2ft. ZONE 8.

TRACHYSTEMON

T. orientale Superb ground cover in dense shade and retentive soil. Makes an important feature with large healthy-looking rough green leaves forming overlapping mounds. Curious blue borage-like flowers in spring, before the leaves take over.
60cm/2ft. ZONE 6.

TRIFOLIUM

T. repens 'Purpurascens Quadriphyllum' This clover is valued for its foliage, mostly

four-leaved, and of a striking chocolate colour. Quickly makes effective ground cover in retentive soil and sun. Typical heads of white clover flowers.
10cm/4in. ZONE 3.

TRILLIUM

Trilliums need deep rich leaf-mould soil, adequate rainfall and cool shady conditions. As the name suggests the parts of the plant are all in threes, three-stemmed leaves, three calyces, three petals.
Trillium grandiflorum Also known as Wake Robin. This is the best known species with pure white flowers.
30–45cm/12–18in. ZONE 5

TROLLIUS

T. europaeus The wild form of Globe-flower is unbeatable with its exquisite pale lemon globes over mounds of glossy cut foliage. Early summer.
75cm/2½ft. ZONE 4.
T. ledebourii (of gardens) Has a mass of orange stamens and slashed petals filling orange bowls. Midsummer.
90cm/3ft. ZONE 5.
T. pumilus Glossy yellow cup-shaped flowers stand on short stems above neat clumps of rich-green divided leaves. Lovely in midsummer on a damp edge, with blue *Myosotis scorpioides* 'Mermaid'.
23cm/9in. ZONE 5.

UVULARIA

U. perfoliata Related to Solomon's Seal, needing retentive leaf-mould soil and part shade. From arching stems dangle light lemon-yellow flowers with long twisting petals held above the leaves in spring. Makes slowly increasing clumps.
30cm/1ft. ZONE 3.

VERATRUM

V. 'Album' Takes 5–7 years to produce good plants from seed. Grow in retentive soil in sun or part shade. A fat tap root produces clusters of hosta-like leaves, finely pleated like a fan. (Guard them from slugs.) In late summer, a tall flower-stem emerges, carrying a pyramidal head of densely set flowers, little white cups shadowed with green.
1.5–2m/4–6ft. ZONE 6.

VERBASCUM

V. chaixii 'Album' White-flowered form, the slender stems tightly packed with flowers with fluffy mauve eyes. Useful vertical for planting among rounded silver-leaved bushes.
75cm/2½ft. ZONE 6.
V. pulverulentum A giant Mullein. Huge rosettes, a yard across, of great grey-white felted leaves. Sends up a tree-like stem covered in white wool, supporting a candelabra-like head of yellow flowers. Biennial. For full sun in well-drained soil. Mid- to late summer.
Over 2m/6–9ft. ZONE 6.

VERBENA

V. bonariensis For hot dry sunny positions with good drainage. Tall rigid branching stems are topped with tightly packed flat clusters of small mauvish scented flowers. Standing high above the silver plants, they make summer screens to view the garden through. Late summer to autumn.
1.5m/5ft. ZONE 8.
V. corymbosa Surprisingly likes moist retentive soil, which it colonizes with tangles of low feathery shoots topped all summer with violet-blue clusters. Useful among *Trollius* or *Rudbeckia* or small bush willows. Flowers for

Veronica teucrium

WALDSTEINIA

W. ternata A beautiful and valuable carpeter which will flourish in retentive soil in sun or part shade, spreading its dark-lobed leaves, evergreen and glossy, to contrast with yellow strawberry flowers in spring. 10cm/4in. ZONE 5.

ZANTEDESCHIA

Z. aethiopica 'Crowborough' The well known Arum Lily, handsome in leaf and flower, grows well in sunny areas in bogs or deeply prepared soil kept moist in summer. Crowns must be protected in winter with heavy mulching. Thrives in deep mud. 90cm/3ft. ZONE 8.
Z. aethiopica 'Green Goddess' Large green flowers with white throats, magnificent foliage. Cultivation as above. 1.5m/4ft plus. ZONE 8.

ZAUSCHNERIA

Z. californica 'Glasnevin' Massed with scarlet tubular flowers for weeks in autumn, this splendid form for sunny well-drained areas, has small matt-green leaves. 38cm/15in. ZONE 8.
Z. cana (californica microphylla) Also known as Humming-bird Trumpet. Will stand the hottest drought. It sends up wiry stems covered with narrow ash-grey leaves, topped in late summer with brilliant scarlet tubular flowers. 30cm/1ft. ZONE 8.

ZIGADENUS

Z. elegans From bulbous plants come grassy leaves while above them stand open spires of pale green, star-shaped flowers, each petal spotted with dark enamelled-green in midsummer. For enriched retentive soil, in sun. 38cm/15in. ZONE 7.

weeks from midsummer. Full sun. 30cm/1ft. ZONE 8.

VERONICA

V. spicata 'Erika' Above compact clusters of grey-green leaves stand dense spires of sugar-pink flowers in midsummer. For sunny areas and retentive soil. 30–38cm/12–15in. ZONE 3.
V. teucrium 'Crater Lake Blue' A good edging plant with low tufts of small green leaves and spires of vivid blue flowers. 30cm/12in. ZONE 3.
V. virginica Valued for its elegant form, creating contrast among mounds and domes of plants. Erect stems, carrying whorls of horizontal dark green leaves, are topped with tapers of tiny close-set flowers, palest pink in late summer. 120cm/4ft. ZONE 3.

VINCA

The periwinkles make excellent evergreen ground cover – in part shade and retentive soil.
V. minor 'Alba' White flowers with small leaves marbled light and dark green in spring and early summer. 20cm/8in. ZONE 5.
V. minor 'Bowles' Blue' This small-leaved, neat-growing periwinkle smothers itself with large blue flowers. Spring. 20cm/8in. ZONE 5.
V. minor 'Variegata' The variegation is green and white, plants smaller. Pale blue flowers. 15cm/6in. ZONE 5.

VIOLA

V. cornuta 'Alba' Long succession of chalk-white flowers in spring and early summer with a late flush in autumn. Prefers full sun and retentive soil. 15cm/6in. ZONE 5.
V. cornuta 'Lilacina' Spreading mats of fresh green foliage covered with china-blue flowers. 15cm/6in. ZONE 5.
V. labradorica Makes a running mass of small dark purple leaves which set off the quantities of light-coloured, scentless flowers. 15cm/6in. ZONE 5.

Plants attractive to bees
Anemone
Aster
Calamintha
Camassia
Campanula
Centaurea
Echinacea
Eryngium
Galtonia
Geranium
Geum
Helleborus
Heuchera
Ligularia
Lythrum
Malva
Petasites
Polemonium
Polygonum
Potentilla
Salvia
Saxifraga
Scabiosa
Sedum
Stachys
Veronica

INDEX

GLOSSARY OF TERMS

The following terms, names and expressions, not all of them horticultural, may well mystify or confuse some American readers, and I have given below either an alternative American word or a brief explanation. The English common plant names used in the text are sometimes better known in the United States by an equivalent American name, and I have included both names in the index, as well as the correct Latin name.

10p piece □ dime

asparagus peas □ edible peapods

buns in a baking tray □ rolls on a cookie sheet

carpeter □ low-level ground cover

chalk, chalk soil □ limestone or alkaline soil

Chelsea Flower Show □ the annual show of the *Royal Horticultural Society* in London in May, opened by HM the Queen. The foremost event in the English gardening calendar. Gold medals are awarded in different categories.

clipping a hedge □ shearing a hedge

cottage garden □ a traditional English garden with a mixture of old-fashioned plants, herbaceous perennials and annuals (and indeed vegetables as well)

cotton wool buds □ cotton twist buds

erica □ heather

half-moon blade □ edging tool

calluna □ heather

Hidcote □ Lawrence Johnston's garden in Gloucestershire

hosepipe □ hose

lawn mowings □ grass clippings

lorries □ trucks

marginal plants □ water's edge plants

marrow □ squash

peastakes □ small twiggy stakes

polythene □ plastic

railway lines □ railroad tracks

ration book □ During and after the Second World War, Britain's food supplies were restricted and everyone carried a ration book entitling them to a quota of certain foods each week.

RHS □ the Royal Horticultural Society, Britain's leading gardening society, founded in the 19th century, and the sponsors of the *Chelsea Flower Show*

runner beans □ pole beans

Sheffield Park □ one of Britain's most impressive arboreta

town gardens □ city yards, gardens

turf □ lawn

William Robinson □ eminent 19th-century English gardener who advocated the use of species plants. Author of several excellent books including *The Flower Garden* and *The Wild Garden*.

PICTURE CREDITS